Working on Cruise Ships

Working on Cruise Ships

Sandra Bow

EDITOR
Susan Griffith

Published by Vacation Work, 9 Park End Street, Oxford

WORKING ON CRUISE SHIPS

by Sandra Bow

Editor Susan Griffith

Copyright © Vacation-Work 1996

ISBN 1 85458 150 3 (softback)
ISBN 1 85458 151 1 (hardback)

Cover Design by
Miller Craig & Cocking Design Partnership

Illustrations by John Taylor

Printed by Unwin Brothers Ltd, Old Woking, Surrey

Contents

INTRODUCTION   11

Why Cruise Lines Need People Like You 11
Facing the Facts: Conceptions and Misconceptions of Life at Sea 11
Applying for a Job – Confirming the Address – The Application Procedure –
Making a Favourable Impression – Interviews – Contracts – Taking the Job –
On-the-Spot Applications 17
What to Expect – Working Hours – Health & Safety – Rules & Regulations –
Dress Code 22
Living Conditions – Accommodation & Food – Seasickness – Leisure –
Chores – Adapting to Life at Sea – Contact with Home –
The Passengers 25
The Hierarchy – Who Wears What? 31
ABC of Jobs at Sea 32
Financial Matters 35
Practical Preparations – Visas & Documents – Joining the Ship –
What to Take 36
The Unofficial Charts: Top Tens for Would-be Mariners 41

ON DECK   44

Opportunities for Deck Officers 44
Training for Deck Cadets 45
Royal Navy 47
Finding a Job in the Deck Department 47
In the Words of a Deck Officer 48

HOTEL DEPARTMENT   50

Some Tips on Tips 50
Purser's Office: – Secretaries – Bookkeepers – Receptionists – Clerks –
PAs 52
In the Words of a Fourth Purser 54

CATERING FOR ALL   55

Jobs in the Restaurant: Maitre d'Hotel – Waiters – Busboys –
Wine Stewards 56
In the Words of a Waiter 56
Jobs in the Kitchen: Chefs – Butchers & Bakers – Catering Ratings – Galley
Assistants – Dishwashers 58

BEHIND BARS   60

Bars Manager – Cocktail Waiters 60
In the Words of a Bartender 60
And Don't Forget the Crew 61
Catering Concessionaires 61

KEEPING THE SHIP SHIP-SHAPE   **62**

Opportunities in Housekeeping at Sea: Chief Steward – Cleaners – Porters – Pantry Stewards – Cabin Stewards 63
In the Words of a Cabin Steward 64
Useful Addresses for Jobs in the Hotel Department 65

OTHER UNUSUAL JOBS AT SEA   **67**

In the Hotel Department – Baggage Masters – Stores Personnel – Garbage Handlers – Concierges – Carpenters – Security Officers – Laundry – Upholsterers 68
Elsewhere on Board – Computer Technicians – Printers – Journalists – Butlers – Port Lecturers – Art Auctioneers – Cruise Sales Manager – Priest – Group Escorts – Florists – Kennel Staff – Bankers 69
In the Words of a Cashier 73

ENTERTAINMENT   **74**

Cruise Staff 75
Childcare Positions – Sample Daily Programme of Children's Activities 76
Sports & Fitness Instructors 79
Technical Assistants 79
Addresses of Cruise Staff Employers 80
In the Words of a Social Hostess 80
In the Words of a Cruise Director 81
Showbusiness: Work for Entertainers, Actors, Dancers, Musicians, Singers, DJs and Magicians 83
Sample Daily Programme 84
Addresses of Entertainment Agencies 88
In the Words of a Dancer 89
What's Your Line?: Opportunities for Experts 90
Jobs for the Boys: Gentlemen Hosts 92
Shore Excursions: Work in the Tour Sector 92

CONCESSIONAIRES   **94**

Retail Shops – Shop Managers – Sales Assistants – Window Dressing   95
Addresses of Shop Concessions 95
In the Words of a Gift Shop Assistant 96
Hair & Beauty Salons – Hairdressers – Beauticians – Manicurists – Masseurs – Chiropodists 97
Spas & Fitness Centres – Gym Staff – Physiotherapists – Aerobics Instructors 98
Addresses of Beauty & Fitness Concessionaires 98
In the Words of a Fitness Instructor 98
Casinos – Croupiers – Cashiers – Pit Bosses – Casino Technicians 99
Useful Contacts for Casino Work 100
In the Words of a Croupier 101
Say Cheese: Opportunities for Photographers – Maritime Photographic Employers 103
In the Words of a Ship's Photographer 104

TECHNICAL & ENGINEERING DEPARTMENT   **106**

Officers – Ratings: Electrical Engineers, Technical & Communications Engineers 107
Training – Recruitment Agencies 108

In the Words of an Engineer 109
The Radio Room – Training 110

MEDICAL TREATMENT   113
Opportunities for Medical Staff – Doctors – Nurses – Medical Orderlies –
Medical Dispensers – Physiotherapists – Dentists 113
In the Words of a Nurse 115

WHICH SHIP?   118
Major Cruise Lines – Cunard – Other Deluxe Lines – Carnival – Disney
Cruises – P & O – RCCL – European Cruise Lines – Theme Cruises 118
How Old? – New Ships – Older Ships 123
How Big? – Large Ships – Small Ships – Mid-Size Ships 125
Sailing Ships & Yachts – Yacht Crewing Agencies 127

CRUISING ITINERARIES – Transatlantic Crossings – Around the World –
Caribbean – Alaska – Mediterranean – Scandinavia and the Baltic – Black
Sea – Far East and Indian Ocean – Hawaii and the South Pacific – Great Barrier
Reef – Bahamas/Bermuda – Central and South America – Rivers – Britain –
Everywhere Else (Expeditions and Speciality Cruises)
– Nowhere (Party Cruises) 129

WHO OWNS THE SHIPS?   135
Alphabetical listing of the cruise companies and the ships they operate 137

CRUISE LINE ADDRESSES   147
Alphabetical listing of major cruise lines, agents and operators worldwide

Cargo and Ferry Company Addresses 160
Other Useful Addresses of Maritime Organisations 162

CRUISE SHIP LISTING   164
Alphabetical listing of cruise ships, showing their operators, usual routes, duration
of cruises, nationality of officers and dining-room staff, passenger capacity and
number of crew members

Appendix 1
Landlubber's Glossary of Nautical Terms 177

Appendix 2
Family Tree of Jobs 182

Appendix 3
Sample Menus for Lunch and Dinner 184

Further Reading 188

Wages throughout this book are quoted in US dollars, since this is the currency
in standard use on all cruise ships. At the time of going to press, the exchange
rate was £1 = US$1.50

Preface

Hundreds of thousands of people dream of taking a cruise. But only a few of them will ever set foot on a luxury liner, and fewer still will actually get paid to do it! And yet there are men and women of all ages and with vastly different skills and experience who have secured enviable positions working on cruise ships, as the opportunities continue to increase. Tourism generally is fast becoming the world's largest industry and cruising is probably the most rapidly expanding sector of it, with many new ships being launched and some of the biggest names in the entertainment world like Disney are looking to increase their involvement.

Some modern cruise ships are really just mobile fun palaces with casinos, cinemas, swimming pools, fitness centres, lecture halls, discos and even golf courses, so the range of jobs is enormous – anything from the usual hotel staff to fortune tellers, florists, gentleman hosts and priests. Wages are generally similar to those on land but the gratuities can be excellent and because most jobs come with full board and lodging the opportunities for saving money are also very good.

In addition of course there are all the well documented opportunities for travel to all corners of the globe, from Alaska to Spitzbergen or Bermuda to Hawaii, and for romance under the glorious sunsets of the Caribbean and Mediterranean. Not so well documented are the long hours and hard work but for me it has all been worthwhile and I am sure will be so for you too. Good luck and *bon voyage.*

Sandra Bow
Cruise Director, *Renaissance VIII*, The Mediterranean
April, 1996

To the memory of John

Introduction

WHY CRUISE LINES NEED PEOPLE LIKE YOU

Cruising is the leisure industry of the nineties. As holidays abroad become accessible to more and more people, tourists are continually searching for new ways of spending their time and money. Cruising — once the preserve of the wealthy — offers a different kind of travel experience which is attracting a wider range of holidaymakers than ever before. As companies compete for the biggest slice of this expanding market, cruising has become a huge growth industry with smaller lines buying more ships, major lines building bigger ships, and all these vessels needing crew members to work on them

Think of a cruise ship as a floating town and you will realise that many of the jobs and skills required on land are also needed at sea. Engineers, cashiers, secretaries, hairdressers, musicians, electricians, croupiers, cleaners, nurses, photographers, waiters, carpenters, shop assistants . . . virtually all walks of life, from auctioneers to zither players, have at one time or another been carried out at sea. The list is endless. And so are the opportunities because, unlike on shore, vacancies occur very frequently.

A large cruise ship may employ over a thousand crew members, many of whom are only at sea for short periods. People move on, settle down, get promoted, fall sick or simply go on leave. Some crew members may use savings earned on ships to set up businesses back home. Others may get married or decide to spend more time with their families. But whatever the reasons, the turnover of employees is enormous.

This, combined with the overall expansion of the industry, means that there are thousands of exciting job opportunities, all ready to be filled by the right person.

FACING THE FACTS

So let's start at the beginning. Why do you want to work on cruise ships in the first place? Is it for the travel? The money? Or just to get out of the rat-race and enjoy life?

You will already have some conceptions of what ship life is like. It is possible that some of these are misconceptions. Here then are some of the more common reasons for going to sea — and the reality behind the myths.

'I want to see the world'

Working on ships is still one of the best ways to see the world. Cruising is a huge industry and most of the major companies have vessels sailing, literally, all over the globe. It should be pointed out, however, that the amount of time you can expect to spend on shore in exotic ports of call will depend greatly on your working schedule. Not all crew members are able to get off at every stop. But even the most overworked seaman or woman can expect to catch a good glimpse of life in foreign lands and will certainly see more of the world than working nine to five in Boringtown.

Of course, if the travel aspect is your main incentive for working at sea, do try and explore as far from the ship's berth as time permits. The dock areas of many, otherwise beautiful, cities can often give a rather sordid first impression, so never judge a port by its port. Also, if you really intend seeing as much as possible of your destination, make a point of venturing ashore with like-minded individuals. Too many 'Jolly Jack Tars' never make it beyond the nearest sleazy bar.

Employees in the staff sector (e.g. gift shops, casino, health and beauty, photography, shore excursions, entertainment/social staff) often have the most free time in port, as in the case of Jim Withers, a 26 year old sports instructor from Merseyside, who admits:

> *Until I started working on cruise ships, I had to save like crazy for every holiday abroad, which was usually nothing more than a ten-day bash with some mates in Benidorm. But in the four years I've been at sea, I've scuba-dived in the Caribbean; water-skied in the Greek Islands; jet-skied in Mexico; parasailed in the Seychelles, and I've actually been paid to do it! Plus, when you consider all the numerous countries I've been lucky enough to visit around the globe, there's no way I could have possibly saved enough by working on land to go to them all. Why earn money to see the world, when you can see the world and earn money at the same time?*

Exactly. Which brings us to. . .

'I want to earn good money'

This is a real possibility although, as with all sectors of employment, salaries vary considerably depending on the type of work you do. Some jobs at sea pay well, often far higher than comparable positions onshore. But you must remember that shipboard earnings cannot be calculated at an hourly rate. Most seamen, irrespective of rank or duties, work long and unsociable hours.

Other jobs may appear to be poorly paid. But don't be put off by a seemingly low basic wage. In general, cruise passengers tip well, and it is not uncommon for an employee's gratuities to exceed the earnings of someone else on a good 'basic'.

The real financial advantage, however, of working at sea is not how much it is possible to earn but how much it is possible to save. There is considerable potential for saving money on cruise ships, largely because the sort of everyday expenses you incur on land are substantially reduced.

Food, accommodation and of course transport are provided, thus eliminating all those shopping, household and car bills. Your laundry is done free (or at a reduced rate) and a drink in the crew bar will almost certainly cost less than in your local.

Some cruise ship stalwarts have become very wealthy, even millionaires, by investing their (often tax-free) earnings wisely. Many employees work at sea for only a few years, before using their savings to facilitate a mortgage, business venture or other financial goal on shore.

Please note that because the American dollar is the most widely used onboard currency, salaries throughout this publication are given first in US dollars, then in British sterling. All salaries and sterling equivalent estimates are very approximate and for guidance only. It is strongly stressed that the renumeration and conditions offered for jobs of the same description really varies greatly from line to line.

You may become the favourite of an aristocratic widow

'I want to work in a cosmopolitan environment'
Cruise ships must be among the most cosmopolitan workplaces imaginable. For economic as well as geographic reasons, cruise lines tend to employ many different nationalities per ship, possibly as many as fifty. And on many cruises the passenger list represents just as much variety.

Note that to overcome stringent registry regulations and, it has to be said, to enable companies to hire 'cheap labour', many ships are registered under 'flags of convenience', mainly Panama, Liberia and Liechtenstein. For example a ship might be registered in Panama though owned by an American company, based in Europe, with mostly Norwegian officers, British staff and Filipino crew. Crazy but frequently true.

They go for the officers first

'I want to rub shoulders with millionaires'

Cruise ship passengers come from all walks of life and it is fair to assume that, especially on longer cruises, you may encounter some very wealthy individuals. Whether you actually rub shoulders (or, indeed, anything else) with them, depends largely on your job on the ship. Social staff have more direct dealings with the passengers than most, but it is not unknown for a barman to become the favourite, or even the husband, of some lonely aristocratic widow. There seem to be more opportunities for male employees than female in this regard, mainly due to the large numbers of unattached ladies on most passenger lists. If a liaison with an ageing millionairess appeals to you, fine. But don't make it your main objective in choosing a career at sea or you may be disappointed.

'I want fun, sun and romance.'

As in other walks of life, being at sea is largely what you make of it. You will probably encounter both fun times and sunny days during your time on the ship, but don't forget that you are planning a working trip and not a vacation. If, after applying for a job as a busboy, you picture yourself sipping champagne in the spa like the models in the glossy brochures, you will definitely be in for a shock. As for romance, the following accounts might provide some insight:

Yes, there's something about cruising that is romantic. It's a holiday atmosphere, and it's easy to get caught up in what are basically holiday romances. People come and go so frequently on ships that lasting relationships are rare. My cabin-mate was heartbroken when her boyfriend disembarked, but within a week she was seeing someone else.

Annie Davies (Casino Cashier)

As a cocktail waiter working in the passenger bars, I suppose you could say I see it all. It seems to me that a lot of young (and also not-so-young) female passengers come onboard obviously looking for romance. Of course they all go for the stripes (officers) first and if they can't get lucky with them they flirt their way down the ranks. I've never understood the attraction of men in uniform but it certainly works. I once knew a DJ who wore his tuxedo even off duty because it was such a hit with the women.

Pedro Parrondo-Sanchez (Cocktail Waiter)

As a female working at sea, especially in the medical department, I am very aware of the level of promiscuity onboard. Some employees can be seen with a different passenger every cruise and a lot of the crew risk sexual disease, including HIV, by frequenting red light areas in foreign ports. I know by the number of cases of VD I treated after our last visit to Thailand!

Vanessa Miller (Nurse)

Having watched The Love Boat, *I was actually disappointed when I first came onboard. I didn't see one dashing officer and half the crew were gay. I ended up seeing guys I would never have dated on land, mainly as company to go ashore. A case of 'Hobson's Choice', really.*

Sylvia Blake (Masseuse)

I wasn't even looking for romance when I joined the ship since I still had a girlfriend back home. But I used to go off onshore with a crowd of the entertainers and, with the best will in the world, it's hard to stay faithful in such exotic locations. I've been seeing Karen (one of the dancers) for over a year now and we intend getting married in June, so I hope this particular shipboard romance will last.

Andrew Savage (Shore Excursions Assistant)

'I want to escape the pressures of work/home/family etc.'
Running away to sea has always been seen as an easy solution to problems at home and in the short-term it can be. Certainly there is a freedom of lifestyle attached to working in a perennially holiday atmosphere. But don't forget that any difficulties, whether personal, marital or financial, will still be waiting for you when you return, and may even have grown more insoluble during your absence. On this note, many crew members find that they end up losing touch with former friends and colleagues while they are away or discover they no longer share the interests of old friends when they return home. Loneliness on shore is an occupational hazard.

Terry Donahue, a gift shop assistant from West Yorkshire, describes his return home on leave:

> *When I first got offered a job in sales at sea, my colleagues in the department store were really pleased for me. A few of them even said they wished they could have got a job on ships too. I sent them the odd postcard and we kept in touch. But the first night that I went down the pub after working nine months in the Caribbean, I found it difficult to keep the conversation going. I'd been away so long I was out of touch with local events — I didn't even know the season's football results — and if I mentioned all the things I did overseas, it appeared as if I was showing off. Although most of my old friends still made me welcome, they didn't want to hear about my travels, and I felt a few people actually resented me for it. In turn, I guess I found their same old life-style boring. It's a shame really, but we seem to have lost that common link.*

'I want a job that's right for me'
Deciding what type of work is exactly right for you is, of course, a very subjective issue. One person's idea of a challenge may be nothing short of a trauma to someone else. An easy workload to some people means pure humdrum to others. But presuming you are prepared to be flexible and have the stamina to endure the frequently long working hours — not to mention the equally long social hours — there is in all likelihood a job at sea that's right for you. While considering the opportunities open to you, concentrate, at least in the first instance, on areas of employment in which you may have some experience.

And a word of advice. If the type of position you'd prefer isn't on offer or seems out of reach at the present time, don't be deterred from accepting a job that you may consider beneath your ability. There are always promotion possibilities on ships, far more than in comparable situations on land. Opportunities often arise unexpectedly, so that capable (and occasionally even incapable) people may suddenly find themselves thrust into a totally different role or department. But much rests on being in the right place at the right time. And the right place is on the ship.

So don't miss the boat.

APPLYING FOR A JOB

After considering the kinds of job for which you might be suited and weighing up the pros and cons of the various cruise lines based on the information in this book, it is time to get down to the business of landing a job at sea (if that isn't a contradiction in terms). As with any form of job hunting, the more possible employers you contact, the better the odds of being accepted. So apply to as many cruise lines, agencies, etc. as possible. Then, should you receive more than one offer of employment, you are in a stronger position to negotiate and/or choose the best terms and conditions. This does not mean, however, that you should not be selective. Do your homework and target companies that you feel are most likely to require your particular skills.

One factor to consider is the minimum age. Most cruise ships are reluctant to hire anyone under 21, though some 18, 19 and 20 year olds have found suitable employment. For work in areas such as bars or casinos you will certainly have to be over 21.

Confirming the Address

The first step in launching your assault on cruise ship companies is to ascertain the correct address of the department which is relevant to the work you are seeking. It is essential to address your application to the appropriate department (preferably using the name of the relevant person) because it is most unlikely that a speculative application will be forwarded to the correct person or even the correct department. Remember too that major cruise lines have offices around the globe and it is no use applying to their UK division for jobs in a particular department if all the recruitment for that line of work is handled in Miami.

When clarifying details, ask for the name and job title of the person to whom you should directly apply and use that name in all correspondence. Your letter will have much more impact than one addressed to an anonymous 'Dear Sir/Madam' or 'Dear Personnel Officer'. (Specific names have not been included in this book since personnel changes in the industry are frequent and such information would soon be out of date). Note that unsolicited faxes are generally considered 'junk mail' and almost invariably hinder rather than help.

Cruise line offices are notoriously busy so it is not surprising that unsolicited telephone calls are not encouraged. Unfortunately, phoning may be the only viable means of obtaining the name and department you need. If you ring at an off-peak time (late afternoon, perhaps) the person answering your call may be more approachable, but be prepared for them simply not to give you the information you require possibly because they don't know it themselves. If this is the case (or you end up talking to an answering machine) then a 'To whom it may concern' via their head office may have to suffice. But whatever reaction you receive from the voice on the line, remember that they are unlikely to have any bearing on your employment prospects and your priority is to get your details to the person who does.

When phoning, don't forget global time differences, e.g. Miami and New York are five hours behind London. To give your prospective employer an alarm call is not a good idea.

The Application Procedure

Having ascertained the name and business address of your target, present your details as professionally as possible. Type (or print out) all communications and always include a covering letter. Set out your CV (resumé) clearly and enclose photocopies of references or other relevant information. Enclose a photograph, preferably one that shows some personality. For jobs in the social/entertainment department a 10 X 8 inch publicity shot is a good bet. Some companies will send you an official form to fill in. If so, don't be afraid to enclose additional information, as long as it is relevant to your application. The more skills and/or qualifications you can offer, the more likely it is that you will be offered a job.

Sometimes you may be offered employment solely on the strength of your application; at other times you may be required to attend an interview. Yet again, you may not even receive a reply. A follow-up telephone call may be beneficial in the latter instance, on the lines of 'I just wanted to make sure you've received my details'. Remind them that you're still alive and waiting. Occasionally it works.

Don't become too disillusioned if you hear nothing. Your details could lie for months in a filing cabinet, only to be dug out and a job offered, requiring you to join a ship in Acapulco in two days time.

Making a Favourable Impression

One busy personnel manager offers some 'dos and don'ts' on preparing to make an application or attend an interview:

> *Too many applicants have obviously not bothered to learn anything about our company or the type of product we are marketing. I get people wanting to work as youth counsellors on vessels that never have children onboard or deal blackjack on ships without a casino. All they had to do was pick up a copy of our brochure and they would have realised that they were wasting their time and ours.*

So what other application 'blunders' does he encounter?

> *Vagueness is very common. It's no use sending in a general 'give us a job' style of letter without any reference to the sector in which you are hoping to find work. Recruitment for each division of a ship, whether housekeeping, entertainment, catering, etc.,*

is handled by a different onshore office or department. If an application arrives without specifying the type of job for which it is intended, the only filing system it's likely to see is the nearest trash can.

Neither are we interested in people who are clearly only looking for a good time with no responsibility or commitment. You would be amazed at the number of applicants who think working on ships is going to be one long holiday and a means of visiting lots of exotic ports, as though the work is incidental. Of course, the travel opportunity is an incentive, and there's nothing wrong with that. But I would be wary of hiring anyone who stressed that angle above, say, their commitment to providing a good service. I've even asked applicants why they wish to work on cruise ships and received unsuitable answers like, 'Well, I've got a few months off and I want to have some fun' or 'I want to be like Julie on the Loveboat' or 'Because I need to get out the country for a while.' Needless to say, they didn't get the job.

What we're looking for is professionalism and commitment. If someone is not smartly dressed at an interview, why should I presume they'll be smartly dressed at work? If someone can't be bothered to show an interest in our company and understand the differences that set us apart from our rivals, why should I think they're going to show any commitment? If someone appears to me as rude or miserable or lacking in confidence, why should I imagine they'll be seen any differently by the passengers? We're really not asking a lot. But you've got to show us that you're the one that we want.

Klaus Kappeler, a bartender from Germany, has recently managed to do just that, by changing his approach:

When I first started trying to get work on ships I was just too honest. I've done a lot of different jobs and I stupidly listed them all in my application, thinking the varied experience would go in my favour. Actually it went against me, because companies thought I was unreliable and wouldn't stick with them for long. So, once I realised this, I adjusted my CV and took out all the jobs that weren't really relevant to the work I was seeking. I've known students looking for vacational work who have also chosen not to tell the whole truth as, understandably, companies are reluctant to employ people who they think are not going to last. It's a case of making your face fit, telling them what they want to hear. Within six weeks of sending off my revised details I had a phone call from Miami offering me a job in the Caribbean.

Interviews

If you are asked to attend an interview, stick to the same kind of rules that you would for any other type of job, that is:

a) Be punctual.
b) Dress smartly and conservatively (definitely no jeans). Over-the-top/ sexy fashion statements and outrageous hairstyles may get you noticed in a nightclub but they won't get you work on a luxury cruise ship.
c) Ask probing questions about the company, about the job, the hours, salary, length of contract, promotion prospects, etc.
d) Be prepared to give answers to standard questions, such as 'Why do you want this particular job?'/'Why do you think you are suited to this type of work?'/'Why did you apply to this particular company?'
e) Establish your personal strengths for the job, i.e. any relevant skills, qualifications or experience, together with factors such as personality, availability and aptitude.

Sexy fashion statements and outrageous hairstyles won't help you get work

Contracts

All cruise lines and reputable agents or employers should issue you with a contract before you start work and this is generally renewed each time you return from leave. As with any contract, read the small print and raise any queries before signing (though this is tricky in the cases when you don't see the contract until you board the ship).

Before signing on the dotted line, you will want to clarify the following points:

a) **Transport.** Will you be expected to travel to the ship at your own expense or will your prospective employer foot the bill? And are you responsible for booking your own flights etc. or will they make the necessary arrangements and reservations for you?

b) **Uniforms.** Are you expected to pay for your own uniforms (if required) or are they provided free of charge? Also, do you need to take uniform items with you or do you pick them up onboard?

c) **Insurance.** Will you be covered by the your employer's insurance or will you need to take out a personal policy? If you are covered, what are you covered for? If it is only for health you may want to insure separately against loss or damage to personal effects.

d) **Tax.** Will your earnings be subject to tax (or other) deductions, or will you be officially self-employed and liable for your own tax declarations?

e) **Payment.** When will you receive your first payment and what form will it take? (cash on the ship, direct credit to a bank account, company cheque, etc.)

f) **Special requirements.** Will you be expected to provide any special items or clothing for your new job? (chef's knives, photographer's cameras, carpenter's tools, evening dress, particular style/colour of shoes, etc.)

g) **Contract conditions.** What are the terms of the contract? How long is it for? Is the full duration of the contract subject to the successful completion of a trial work period?

h) **Commission.** Are you liable to pay commission on your earnings and, if so, for how long? Note that some agencies include contractual clauses, demanding commission on extended or follow-up contracts or additional offers of work, even if they have absolutely nothing to do with setting up the ensuing contract and you have procured it independently.

i) **Any other expenses.** Will there be any hidden expenses that you have not been told about (e.g. a deduction for food and accommodation)?

Since the demise of unions in the merchant fleet, it should be stressed that many ships' contracts are barely worth the paper they are written on. There is little, if any, job security at sea. But this works both ways: while it is relatively easy for companies to break their side of the bargain, neither are they likely to rush straight to the law courts if you should happen to break yours.

If you are told that your contract won't be available until you board the ship, be sure to obtain a letter or document (even a fax copy) from your future employer, stating the date you are to commence work and the vessel you will be joining. Carry this with you when passing through foreign immigration as proof of your reason for entering the country where you are due to pick up the ship. This particularly applies if you are a non-US citizen entering the United States.

Taking the Job

This brings us to the vital subject of availability. Cruising, more than any other, is an industry where 'he who hesitates is definitely lost'. So if a job is offered at short notice (and presuming you are reasonably happy with the terms and conditions), take it. Even if it means dropping everything and flying to Honolulu, take it. And even if you are not quite sure what you are letting yourself in for, take it. Because if you don't take it, such an opportunity may never be offered to you again. So much in cruising depends on being in the right place (or being available to get to the right place) at the right time.

On-the-Spot Applications

The old-fashioned approach of asking at the gangway for an impromptu interview might work if you happen to live in a port town and are prepared to spend your time loitering around the docks. Ships that frequent ports as part of a regular itinerary may be especially interested in taking on local crew members, particularly if they are inadvertently caught short-staffed, as it may be cheaper and more convenient than recruiting elsewhere. Personal contacts or recommendations will obviously help your case, but be prepared for rejections and referrals.

WHAT TO EXPECT

If you are in the financial position to take a holiday abroad, why not plan a cruise as your next vacation? It is often possible to book a cruise for not much more than other types of package holiday, and it would at least give you an insight as to what to expect. During the course of your vacation, you would have the opportunity to talk first-hand to those already working onboard, and you might even make some useful contacts for future employment.

Those who are heading for their first contract at sea will no doubt be anxious about what life will be like. This section provides answers to some of the most commonly asked questions about working conditions first and then living conditions.

Q: How long will I work at a time?
A: Again, this really depends on your job on the ship and the particular cruise line. If you are having to pay your own transport costs you will naturally want to work for as long a stretch as possible instead of flitting home every other month. If, on the other hand, the company is paying your costs, you may want to take regular leave. The minimum stretch of work for regular employees (as opposed to visiting entertainers, etc.)

is usually about three months, although some crew members may choose to work for up to a year without a break. With the exception of personnel on officer contracts, most members of a ship's company are officially self-employed and are therefore not paid when on leave.

Q: Will I get a day off?
A: Very unlikely. Irrespective of your position on the ship (with the possible exception of certain members of the entertainment department) you will be required to work every day. Of course, you will have time off, maybe whole mornings, afternoons or evenings, as the case may be. But most crew members work long and often anti-social hours, seven days a week.

Q: What if I have an accident or fall ill?
A: The cruise line will usually cover any medical costs for accidents, injuries or general illnesses of ship's personnel, whether incurred on or off-duty, at sea or on land, as long as the crew member is in the ship's service at the time (i.e. has 'signed on' as all crew members must do on joining or re-joining a ship). When an employee leaves a ship (even to go on leave with the intention of returning), he or she signs off and is no longer covered by the company's insurance.

While in service, crew members are entitled to the ship's medical services free of charge and may even be admitted to the ship's hospital for a short recuperation period. Nevertheless if you require medication for an ongoing condition, take a supply with you rather than assume that the ship's pharmacy will have what you need in stock.

If an employee becomes so ill or is so seriously injured that he/she is unable to fulfill his/her contract and has to return home or be admitted to a shoreside hospital, the company is unlikely to pay treatment charges and (in most cases) is not liable for sickness pay. It must be stressed that this is an area of great discrepancy and it is well worth checking on a company's medical policies before accepting a contract. Better still, take out a personal insurance policy that will also give you travel cover. In the United Kingdom, Marcus Hearn & Co (65-66 Shoreditch High St, London E1 6JL; tel 0171-739 3444) offer a policy which covers people who intend working overseas, as opposed to simply taking a vacation.

Q: Will I receive special safety training?
A: Obvious risks such as fire, stormy weather, collisions and flooding are ever-present when working at sea. Specialist training to enable crew members to cope with the eventuality of life-threatening situations is a priority of all reputable cruise lines.

Generally, all new crew members will be requested to attend a safety course within a short time of joining the vessel. This course should cover emergency procedures, lifeboat/raft instruction and basic firefighting. In addition, all crew members will be expected to attend regular crew safety drills and some will also be requested to assist with the passenger safety drills. It should be pointed out that in the course of these (particularly crew) drills you may be expected to assist in physical, grimy and even potentially dangerous activities which you may consider irrelevant to the job for which you were hired. Manicurists and ballroom dancers be warned.

Ships sailing out of American ports also have to pass both stringent US coastguard inspections (which affect all crew members) and United States Public Health (USPH) inspections of all hygiene and sanitation arrangement (which involve a great number of the crew).

It is advisable to familiarise yourself with the emergency routes from your cabin and workplace as soon as possible after joining a ship. Make sure you can quickly locate the water-tight and fire doors, and also learn how to use the fire extinguishers and launch the lifeboats/rafts. This is not just to satisfy the US coastguards but for your own peace of mind, so that you will know how to bail yourself out if those designated to help you are nowhere to be found.

Q: Are there many rules and regulations?
A: Naturally, there will be certain rules and regulations. Some ships are much harder to work on than others in this respect. It is fair to assume that whatever your rank you will be bound by rules concerning appearance, time-keeping and conduct. Some companies may even operate a penalty system, whereby employees are financially penalised or refused shore leave for misdemeanours.

Certain areas of the ship may be out of bounds, depending on your job and rank, and permission to socialise in passenger areas may be subject to not occupying bar stools or sitting in large groups of staff members. Perhaps the least popular rule to be enforced on some ships is the curfew system, whereby all off-duty employees other than senior officers must vacate the passenger areas by a specified time at night.

Any crew member amassing several verbal or written warnings for offences is liable to be dismissed, as is anyone unfortunate enough to miss the ship without a very good excuse. Drunkenness, swearing and fighting, particularly in passenger areas, will nearly always result in dismissal, especially if your opponent was higher ranking than you.

If getting fired seems to be something of an occupational hazard, getting re-hired, possibly by another cruise line within the same week, may come just as easily. Your claim of 'unfair dismissal' will almost certainly fall on deaf ears, but your new employer may not ask too many questions either.

Suffice to say, most of the regulations appear worse on paper than they do in practice, and in the unlikely event that you do face disciplinary action, take consolation in the knowledge that, unlike your predecessors, you won't be flogged at dawn.

Q: What should I wear?
A: All officers, staff and crew members wear the uniform allocated to their job when on duty, with the exception of entertainers and social staff members who wear their own clothes for certain occasions like

cocktail parties. In the evenings, ship's personnel not in uniform should adhere to the passenger dress code, which may range from very formal to casual, depending on the nature of events. Note, however, that even 'casual' does not include T-shirts or jeans, unless of course it happens to be Wild West Night.

Typical evening dress codes for the passengers and non-uniformed employees are:

Formal — Evening/cocktail dress for women, tuxedo/evening suit (black tie) for men

Informal — Dress/suit for women, business suit/jacket and tie for men

Casual — Dress/trousers for women, collared shirt (no jacket/tie required) for men

Theme — Dress appropriate to the theme, e.g. 50s/60s, Black & White, Tropical, Country & Western, etc.

Uniformed officers will also be expected to follow the evening dress codes, wearing dress uniform on formal nights. Your company will advise you of their requirements.

Most officers and many crew members are expected to buy the uniforms required for their job. However, policies on uniforms vary considerably from company to company and some lines will provide good quality uniforms free of charge. Do check on this before accepting a job offer, as uniform costs may eat into your profits, particularly if you are not looking for a long-term career. Footwear is not provided and there may be certain stipulations, such as shoe colour or heel height. In the main, however, common sense prevails, especially bearing in mind that many crew members spend long hours on their feet.

Additional regulations may concern hair styles (particularly for those handling food) and general appearance (no earrings for male employees, for instance).

Naturally, during your free time and on trips ashore you may wear whatever you like, although it should be noted that most cruise lines are averse to personnel wearing jeans or cut-away shorts in passenger areas even in their free time.

LIVING CONDITIONS

Q: What will my accommodation be like?

A: Your accommodation will depend on the status given to your particular job and the ship on which you are working. Officers and other senior employees will generally have single accommodation with en-suite shower/toilet facilities. Accommodation for staff (and this includes casino, health & beauty and shop concessionaires) is variable and may be single or shared, depending on your job and the cabin allocation for your department. Managerial and 'one-off' positions generally warrant good standard single accommodation with en-suite facilities, while other staff positions may involve sharing with one or (rarely) two other employees (usually of the same department). Some staff members and entertainers may be allocated passenger accommodation, and often these are cabins that for reasons of location, noise, etc., would be difficult to sell but are nevertheless quite acceptable.

Cabins allocated to crew — i.e. non-managerial restaurant and bar staff, cabin stewards and 'ratings' — are often shared by two to four people (usually of the same department) subject to space availability. Crew accommodation on newer ships tends to be superior to that on older ones.

Possibly the best crew accommodation currently afloat can be found on the *Europa* (Hapag-Lloyd) and the *Crystal Harmony* and *Crystal Symphony* (belonging to Crystal Cruises). Other ships with good crew quarters include the *Queen Odyssey* (RCL), the *Asuka* (NYK), the *Royal Viking Sun* (Cunard Line) and the *Seabourn Pride* and *Seabourn Spirit* (Seabourn Cruise Line).

Q: What about the food?
A: Again, your dining place will be subject to your rank or job status. Officers usually eat in the Officers' Mess with waiter service while crew members dine in the self-service Crew Mess. Staff members, entertainers and concessionaires have the most variable allocations, depending on the ship. Larger ships may have a Staff Mess with waiter-service or self-service while smaller ships may reserve a section of a passenger restaurant for staff. Officers and staff members are usually permitted to eat at passenger buffets as long as they don't queue jump. Certain senior officers and members of the social/entertainment sector may also be expected to host a passenger table for dinner on specified evenings.

While passenger food is of a reasonable to excellent standard, crew food can be variable even on the best of ships. So if you get a good deal (and crew food can be good) eat well, as tomorrow you may prefer to diet.

Q: What if I get seasick?
A: If you are generally prone to travel sickness, it may be a good idea to take some form of remedy until you find your sea legs. Medication is usually freely available on board, but if you still find yourself suffering:
a) Try to get fresh air. Go out on the deck if you can and look out at the horizon, not down at the waves. Alternatively, keep to the middle of the ship and on as low (and therefore stable) a deck as possible.
b) Eat dry salted crackers and non-greasy foods. Generally, avoid alcohol, although it must be said that an occasional 'stabilizer' (combination of port and brandy) has helped many a sea dog regain his swagger.
c) Concentrate on some activity or busy yourself to take your mind off the nausea. Try and work through it; you may have no choice.

Above all, don't let the prospect of seasickness put you off working on ships. Many of the most popular routes tend to be in calmer waters and it is not a myth that even so-called bad sailors get better over a period of time.

Q: What leisure facilities are there for the crew?
A: Generally, the bigger the ship, the better the facilities for crew members. Larger ships may have a crew gymnasium, sunbathing area,

library and even specialist facilities such as a computer centre. Most ships will have a Crew Bar and/or Recreation Room, although bar opening hours may be subject to restrictions.

Crew facilities are important on a ship, since crew members (and this includes waiters and bar staff) are not usually allowed in passenger areas except to work. The ship's officers will probably have a Ward Room (Officers' Bar) and officers generally have access to all (certainly, most) public rooms, including (discretional) use of the passenger pool, sauna, gymnasium, etc. Staff, entertainers and certain concessionaires also have public rooms privileges (these vary from ship to ship) and on larger vessels they may also have their own Bar or Recreation Room.

Q: Do I have to do my own cleaning?
A: Officers, staff members, entertainers and other members of the ship's company will be allocated a cabin steward(ess) to attend to the general cleaning and servicing of cabins (but not necessarily tidying). Although the steward's wages are usually paid by the company, good service should be rewarded with a tip.

Lower ranking crew members are generally responsible for the cleaning and servicing of their own cabins, although a small fee may well secure the assistance of one of the cabin stewards. (In fact, ship-wise employees soon learn that an odd backhander or service bartered can considerably improve the quality of life in all areas of work and accommodation). Towels and bed linen are supplied and laundered free of charge by the ship.

The cabins of all personnel, even senior officers, may be subject to frequent inspections. The main purpose of these is not to snoop into your personal belongings but to ensure against risks caused by vermin, structural damage and fire hazards.

Q: What about my laundry?
A: Most ships will have self-service laundry facilities especially for the ship's personnel. (It must be said, however, that the condition of some of the washing machines and dryers leaves a lot to be desired). Crew members' uniforms and overalls are usually cleaned free of charge by the ship's laundry service and there are generally special rates for personal items sent to the onboard laundry.

Q: Will I be able to adapt to my new surroundings?
A: This is something you will never know until you step aboard your first ship. Everyone finds things hard for those first few days, even seasoned crew members joining a new vessel. But whether or not you take to the lifestyle and enjoy it or are tempted to disembark at the next port really depends on you.

Joining a ship for the first time can be hard, especially if you've never really been away from home or travelled that much before. What makes it especially difficult is the fact it's not just a new job, it's a whole new lifestyle.

You may find your working hours a lot longer and less social than before. Then at the end of a hard day you might have to share a cabin with someone you don't know and possibly don't even like. You can't get away from your colleagues like you can on land. You can't just go home at five o'clock, put the kettle on and forget about work. You may not be able to get off the ship for days at a time. There might be more petty rules and regulations than you've been used to, the food may be lousy, you feel institutionalised and you're missing your family or partner back home. These are all things that newcomers find difficult to handle.

Plus, it's easy to become burnt out, not only by the work but also because experiences and emotions are heightened by being permanently in transit. There's far less stability at sea than onshore. People come and go. You make friends and live with them for 24 hours a day for several months, then they get off and you never see them again. The same with relationships. Tearful farewells are more commonplace at sea than on land. What could be more dramatic or poignant than sailing out of port, while your disembarked lover stands, suitcase in hand, on the pierside?

Even ordinary activites like going to a bar or hiring a jeep are much more exciting in a strange and foreign country. You become more streetwise, more self-sufficient. But so much depends on the individual. Ship life tends to suit people who are independent and a bit adventurous, but I would say to anyone with doubts, 'Try it'. Whether it will be the best time or the worst time of your life — and it will probably be both — the main thing is having the guts to walk up the gangway.

Jonathon Globerman (Crew Purser)

Q: How can I maintain contact with home?
A: Receiving news from home is a highlight for most employees on cruise ships. Your family or friends can write to you via your company head office where crew mail is then forwarded to the ship through worldwide port agents. Alternatively, mail may be sent directly to the port agents (addresses are available from the Crew Purser). It must be stressed, however, that some port agents are better than others at passing on crew mail. Be sure to tell contacts to mark all correspondence very clearly with your name, rank/position and the name of your ship, and advise them not to send you valuable items unless absolutely necessary. You will generally be able to send mail from the ship's onboard postbox (to be posted ashore by agents shortly after sailing). In emergencies, you can make and receive telephone calls round-the-clock via the ship's satellite. But this is an expensive option for routine conversations and most crew members phone home from shoreside phones or calling stations.

You may also want to consider taking members of your family onboard. A temporary visitors' pass is usually all that is required to allow family members and friends on to visit. If you wish to have relatives staying onboard, then special cruising rates normally apply. Some cruise companies offer very good deals for family members and, subject to your rank and length of service, your next-of-kin may even travel free for a specified time. It is generally not possible, however, for family members, spouses or children to remain onboard for more than a vacation (unless, of course, they are also employees).

Q: What will the passengers be like?

A: Of course, there is one factor common to every single cruise ship and every single cruise line, and that is the passengers. Cruise ship passengers come in a variety of shapes and sizes but, in spite of recent successes in attracting a wider family market, most cruisers still fall into the 'Fair, Fat and Forty (Plus)' category. Pity then the poor steward who, when asked to assist a gentleman trying to find his wife, was told to look for a lady who was 'short and plump, with grey hair and glasses,' a description that could easily have fitted the majority of females on the guest list.

Many passengers may also be spending their retirement nest egg, which is possibly one of the reasons why cruising is one of the few industries not to have been badly affected by recent economic recessions.

Vincent Ardito, a 68 year old regular cruiser from Philadelphia explains why he keeps coming back:

> *The way I see it, my wife and I have worked hard all our lives and we deserve to enjoy our retirement. When we were younger we couldn't afford to travel. We were too busy bringing up a family and paying the bills. Now the kids have families of their own and we've got a lot of catching up to do.*

But why take a cruise as opposed to any other type of vacation? Doris Campbell, from Essex, England, would never consider anything else:

> *I first took a cruise with my sister the year after my husband died, and I've travelled on 16 cruises since. What I like most is the convenience. You visit umpteen different countries and yet you only unpack once. And because your transport is also your hotel, you can leave all your valuables safely onboard when you go ashore. On the ship, everything is so handy. Whether you attend a lecture, swim in the pool or browse in the shops, it's all just a deck or two away. And there's so much to do that I'm never bored.*
>
> *But the main pleasure for me is the evening's entertainment. I love watching the shows and listening to the classical concerts. I also enjoy ballroom dancing, but all the dance halls back home are gone now, so it's wonderful to be able to dance onboard to a proper big band. I tend to choose ships that have gentlemen hosts as they always make good partners, with no strings attached. As*

an older single woman, I wouldn't feel comfortable going out alone at night on land. But at sea, I can dance the night away, go in any of the bars, watch a film or show on my own, and not have to worry about getting back to my hotel. I feel safe on the ship. It's a sort of home from home.

Considering factors such as rough weather, steep gangways and the use of tender boats, it is somewhat surprising that cruising proves so attractive to many physically-challenged passengers, with an increasing number of ships offering facilities such as wheelchair-accessible cabins. Less surprisingly, it is also the dream vacation for romantics, would-be romantics, honeymooners and those celebrating anniversaries or other special occasions.

But while lovers may stroll the decks under the same old moon, for those who remember the age of the great liners, cruising just 'ain't what it used to be'.

Tony Andrews, a Chief Steward of some 20 years experience, reflects:

Oh yes, cruising has changed. It used to be an elegant experience, attracting the cream of society. Now, everyone and anyone takes a cruise. Standards have dropped enormously, but it's inevitable because what used to be reserved for the elite is now a mass market tourist industry, a change for which the cruise lines themselves are responsible. They keep building bigger and bigger ships that hold so many passengers, it's impossible to maintain the kind of personal service that we used to give.

In addition, they offer really cheap deals in order to fill all those empty cabins, hoping that the passengers will spend, spend, spend once onboard. Some of them do, but a lot are just cheap-skates. And it's always the ones who have paid the least who complain the most. We get couples paying next-to-nothing for a ten-day holiday, which includes round-the-clock service, food and entertainment, and they do nothing but moan about the fact that they don't get caviar or fresh lobster every meal. You feel like telling them that if they were at home they'd be lucky to get bed & breakfast for the price.

Unfortunately, I feel the tendency for customers to demand more for less is something that affects not only cruising, but the whole tourism industry. They all like to think that they are sophisticated travellers, but fewer people dress appropriately for dinner any more, and the ones who do will often change into 'something more comfortable' straight afterwards, which means you frequently see passengers wandering around in T-shirts on formal nights.

Yes, it's definitely the end of an era, but we all have to come to terms with the changes in the industry. When I'm faced with a particularly tricky customer, I don't let it get to me. Instead, I remind myself that, in spite of everything, I'm still earning a very good living at their expense.

THE HIERARCHY

On the majority of ships there are three categories of employee and this hierarchy creates a marked class system: officer, staff and crew. Officers (from fourth pursers up) are free to make use of all ship facilities and enjoy superior living quarters. 'Staff' consist of shop staff, hairdressers, beauticians, casino staff and others working for concessionaires (explained later). The lowest rung is 'crew' whose leisure activities are more circumscribed (socialising may be confined to the 'crew bar') and whose living quarters may be cramped and spartan especially on older ships, with four sharing a small cabin in the least desirable part of the ship. The redeeming feature of this system is that there is usually scope for promotion, although crew members have been known to turn down promotion if it means losing out on tips.

Who Wears What?

Maritime officers wear stripes on their epaulets or the base of their jacket sleeves to denote their rank. The colour (if any) between the stripes and optional accompanying symbol signifies their department of work, according to the following traditional guidelines:

Deck — No colour — Diamond
Hotel — White — Clover leaf
Technical & Engineering — Purple — Propeller
Electrical — Purple — Electric Current
Medical — Red — Caduceus (i.e. staff of Hermes)
Communications — Green — Radio signal
Security — Brown — 'S'

While it must be stressed that different cruise lines do not always allocate the same status to jobs of the same title, this listing may serve as a general guide:

Four Stripes:
Captain
Chief Engineer
Hotel Manager
Staff Captain
Staff Chief Engineer

Three Stripes:
Assistant Hotel Manager
Chief Electrician
Chief Officer
Chief Radio (Communications) Officer
Cruise Director (although the CD may never actually wear them)
Executive Chef
Food & Beverage Manager

Medical Officer (Doctor)
Purser

Two and a Half Stripes:
Assistant Food & Beverage Manager
Assistant (Hotel/Crew) Purser
Bars Manager
Chief Security Officer
Chief Steward
Deputy Cruise Director
First Officer (Deck, Engineering, etc.)
Housekeeper

Two Stripes:
Nurse
Second Officer (Deck, Engineering, etc.)
Second Purser

One and a Half Stripes:
Senior Secretary
Third Officer (Deck, Engineering, etc.)
Third Purser

One Stripe:
Cadet
Fourth Officer (Deck, Engineering, etc.)
Fourth Purser
Petty Officer

Note that high-ranking staff members, such as shop, casino or beauty salon managers, chefs, maitre d's and senior social staff personnel may often have officer status and privileges, even though they don't actually wear stripes.

It may be easier to appreciate the different degrees of status attached to particular areas of work by considering the employment structure of the ship as a whole. Turn to page 182 for a typical cruise ship's 'Family Tree of Jobs'.

ABC OF JOBS AT SEA

Let's go back to basics and identify the types of work opportunities that exist on cruise ships. In later chapters, we will be looking at the jobs themselves, their requirements, their availability and how to apply for them. But first, check out the range of possibilities. There are about 200 of them listed below, and the list is far from exhaustive.

Most jobs at sea fall into one of four categories: Deck, Hotel (including Catering, Concessions and Entertainment), Technical and Engineering (including Electrical and Communications), and Medical. Each of these departments offers a great many different job opportunities, all of which are discussed later in the book.

You may have already considered some of the jobs. Others you may not have even thought of. But all of these jobs can be found at sea. As you go down the list, it is to be hoped that you will discover at least one or two job titles that appeal. Bear them in mind for future reference. It will make selecting your potential job as easy as ABC.

The following jobs are available to both men and women, at least in theory. Titles such as manager, actor, director, masseur, etc. do not assume a gender preference.

Able Seaman (AB)
Accommodation Services Manager
Accountant
Actor
Aerobics Instructor
Art Auctioneer
Assistant Bar Manager
Assistant Cruise Director
Assistant Food & Beverage/
    Catering Manager
Assistant Hotel Manager
Assistant Housekeeper
Assistant Maitre d'
Assistant Manager (Shop, Spa, etc.)
Assistant Purser
Assistant Steward

Baggage Master
Baker
Ballroom Dancer
Banker
Bar Steward
Bars Manager
Bar Waiter
Beautician
Beauty Salon Manager
Bellman
Berthing Officer
Bookkeeper
Bosun
Buffet Chef
Busboy
Butcher
Butler

Cabin Steward
Captain
Carpenter
Cashier
Casino Manager

Head Wine Steward
Host/ess
Hotel Manager
Hotel Purser
Housekeeper

Inspector (Casino)
International Host/ess

Joiner
Journalist
Junior Officer (Deck, Radio,
    Purser, Engineering, etc.)

Kennel Hand

Laundry Assistant
Laundry Master
Librarian

Magician
Maitre d'
Manicurist
Manifest Officer
Masseur
Medical Dispenser
Medical Orderly
Motorman
Musical Director
Musician

Navigator
Nurse
Nursery Assistant

Office Clerk
Officer Cadet (Deck, Engineering,
    etc.)
Opera Singer
Ordinary Seaman (OS)

P.A. (Personal Assistant)
Pantry Steward

Casino Technician
Catering Assistant
Catering Manager
Chef de Cuisine
Chef Entremetier
Chef de Partie
Chef de Rang
Chief Electrician
Chief Engineer
Chief Officer
Chief Photographer
Chief Radio Officer
Chief Security Officer
Chief Steward
Children's Counsellor
Chiropodist
Choreographer
Classical Musician
Cleaner
Cocktail Pianist
Cocktail Waiter
Commis Chef
Communications Engineer
Computer Technician
Concert Pianist
Concierge
Crew Purser
Croupier
Cruise Director
Cruise Sales Manager
Cruise Staff Member

Dancer
Deck Carpenter
Deck Officer
Deckhand
Dentist
Deputy Cruise Director
Disc Jockey
Dishwasher
Doctor

Electrical Assistant
Electrician
Engineer
Engineering Assistant
Entertainer
Executive Chef

Pastry Chef
Photographer
Physiotherapist
Pit Boss (Casino)
Plumber
Port Lecturer
Porter
Priest
Principal Medical Officer
Printer
Programme Co-ordinator
Public Rooms Manager
Purser

Quartermaster

Rabbi
Radio Officer
Radio Room Assistant
Rating (Non-officer: Catering, Deck, Hotel, etc.)
Receptionist (Purser's)
Restaurants Manager

Safety Officer
Sales Assistant
Sauce Chef
Secretary
Security Officer
Second Officer (Deck, Radio, Purser, Engineering, etc.)
Senior Nurse
Ship's Service Manager
Shop Manager
Shore Excursions Assistant
Shore Excursions Manager
Singer
Social Director
Social Hostess
Sound/Lighting Engineer
Sous Chef
Spa Assistant
Spa Manager
Sports Director
Staff Captain
Staff (Deputy) Chief Engineer
Stage Manager
Stage Technician
Stores Assistant

First Officer (Deck, Radio, Purser, Engineering etc.)
Fitness Instructor
Florist
Food & Beverage/Catering Manager
Fourth Officer (Deck, Radio, Purser, Engineering, etc.)

Galley Assistant
Garbage Handler
Gardener
Gentleman Host
Group Escort
Guest Lecturer/Expert (e.g. Archaeologist, Arts & Crafts, Astrologer, Astronomer, Bridge, Cartoonist, Celebrity Speaker, Finance, Gardening, Golf, Hand-writing Analyst, Palmist, Self-improvement, Tarot Card Reader, and so on)
Gymnasium Supervisor

Hairdresser
Harpist
Head Chef
Head Waiter

Stores Manager

Tailor
Technical Engineer
Television Station Manager
Third Officer (Deck, Radio, Purser, Engineering, etc.)

Unskilled Assistant (Catering, Office, etc.)
Upholsterer

Variety Artist
Vegetable Chef

Waiter
Water Sports Instructor
Wine Steward

Xylophonist

Youth Counsellor

Zither Player

Is there anything listed that might be suitable for you? If so, you will need to know more about the type of work for which you are aiming. To find out more about the specific departments and their requirements, we'll take each one step by step, deck by deck.

FINANCIAL MATTERS

One of the most important issues to consider is whether or not you have to pay your own travel expenses to join the ship. Officers, entertainment staff and senior personnel will generally have their flights and travelling expenses paid for and arranged by the company. Concessionaires may have their expenses paid and arranged by the companies that employ them. But the majority of the crew will have to pay, at least in the first instance, for their own transport to and from the ship. Some cruise companies have a policy of paying a percentage of flight costs or reimbursing travelling expenses after a fixed period, but it really does vary from line to line, which is another good reason to shop around if you are in a position to do so. Whatever the situation should be specified in your contract. Cruise lines tend to start off the way they mean to go on, so that those which cover transport and uniform costs tend to be more generous employers in all respects.

Many people wonder whether they will have to contribute towards food and accommodation. Sometimes, staff members who are employed by an independent concessionaire do have some deductions made for living expenses. But the vast majority of employees receive free food and accommodation, while senior officers and social staff members may even receive an additional drinks allowance.

On this subject: 'Health Warning: Working at sea can seriously damage your liver.' Alcohol on passenger ships is cheap (or even 'on the house') and very available and it is no coincidence that a high ratio of employees become heavy social drinkers.

With the exception of certain senior officers, most ship's personnel are paid in cash (usually twice a month and often in American dollars) by the Crew Purser on the ship. Many ships also offer crew banking facilities to transfer payment or to arrange for a portion of the salary to be automatically sent to a home account. Members of the ship's company who are employed by an organisation or agent other than the cruise line may be paid independently (by cheque or direct credit) by their employer.

The tax situation for people working at sea is generally very favourable. Since most ships are registered in tax haven countries and also because many crew members are classified as self-employed, tax is seldom withdrawn at source. Rather, you will be personally responsible for declaring your earnings to the tax office (or not, as the case may be). British seafarers must work at sea for at least one full tax year (April 6th — April 5th) and stay out of the United Kingdom for at least six months at a time to be eligible for tax exemption. There are plenty of tax exiles currently working at sea, but don't presume a three month contract in the Baltic will save you from the Bogey Man.

PRACTICAL PREPARATIONS

Visas and Documents

Obviously you will need a full passport and, subject to the route your particular ship is taking, you may need visas to visit certain countries. Generally, this is not a problem, and any necessary visas will be arranged for the crew by the Crew Purser in conjunction with local officials in each port.

If you are sailing to or from American ports and you are not a US citizen you will definitely need a Seaman's Visa (C-1/D). This is available from US Embassies and is valid for five years from the date of issue. To obtain your C-1/D, you will need to supply written proof (such as a contract) of an offer of employment at sea. If in doubt, check with your prospective employer.

Don't forget to check if you will be stopping at any ports in countries which require a vaccination certificate, which normally only arises if you have been to countries in which yellow fever is prevalent. Also, most cruise lines will request proof of a recent successful medical examination and some may also require you to submit results of an HIV test. If there is insufficient time to undergo a medical examination before you join the ship, you will probably be required to have one on board. Be aware that a history of epilepsy, mental disorder, heart disease or other major illness could seriously impair your chances of employment at sea.

Joining the Ship

Crew change-overs usually take place on the same day as passenger change-overs (with predictably chaotic results), with most employees joining their ship at its base port. An exception to this would be when a 'handover' period is required, usually in the case of senior personnel where some overlap is required for the new employee to learn the ropes from the outgoing employee or to ensure continuity. If this is the case, employees may be asked to embark days or even weeks before assuming their positions of responsibility. Most lower ranks learn the ins and outs of their jobs while actually doing it.

On this note, don't expect a 'settling in' period or a chance to recuperate from jet lag. Whatever your rank, you will probably have to start work as soon as you arrive, sometimes even before you unpack, and this can come as a shock after a long gruelling journey. Cruise ship employees frequently cover almost as many miles by air as they do by sea and unless you are fortunate enough to be embarking in a local port, you will probably have to fly half way round the world to join your ship.

If your cruise line arranges your travel, do not expect a convenient journey. In order to save a little money, you may be put on flights with different airlines with badly timed connections which may necessitate a stopover in some obscure hotel miles from the airport. The cruise lines do not seem to take into consideration that after paying for the cost of your overnight accommodation and the taxi fare trying to find it, they could have flown you directly to your ship for less money. But that's cruise lines for you.

On arrival at your destination you should be met by a ship's representative, such as their port/shipping agent, who will escort you to the vessel. Sometimes, because of flight arrangements, you may arrive the day before the ship is due, in which case the agent will arrange overnight accommodation and transport you to the ship in the morning. It should be stressed that despite assurances to the contrary things do not always run according to plan. The most common problems, together with their suggested solutions, are as follows:

a) There is no-one to meet you at your destination.

Phone the ship's agent to collect you from the airport. If you arrive in the middle of the night, check into a convenient hotel (it is not unknown for abandoned employees travelling on company expenses to select the most expensive, 'inadvertently' of course) and then contact the cruise line or ship's agent in the morning. If you have to make your own way to the ship, take a taxi and keep receipts of any expenses for reimbursement.

b) Your luggage goes missing.

Make sure you give the airport officials all details, including contact numbers of your cruise line and their local shipping agent and the name of your intended ship. Inform your cruise line and/or the ship's agent of the situation, as they can help to follow things up on your behalf. With luck your luggage will be forwarded to the vessel at the next convenient port of call (see also below *What to Take*).

c) You miss your sailing.

If you are delayed by Customs or Immigration officials through no fault of your own, try to get a message to your cruise line or their shipping agent, as sometimes they can help resolve immigration problems. If you miss the ship because of such delays, the agent should make the necessary arrangements for you to join the vessel at the next convenient port.

If you miss the ship at any time during your sea-going career, the local ship's agent can help you to pick it up again, even though you will almost invariably be responsible for flights, accommodation and any other costs incurred. Missing the ship can be an expensive mistake; it may even cost you your job. Always check the 'All Aboard' time before going ashore.

And while ashore, be warned that ship's crew members are often seen as easy prey for dealers of drugs and other contraband. However much you may stand to gain, bear in mind that cruise lines are universally stringent in their rules on illegal drugs and that some countries even equip their ports with armed militia and sniffer dogs. If you are caught smuggling illegal substances or goods, not only will your job be on the line, but you may find yourself at the mercy of a foreign (and possibly corrupt) legal system, and in a country where the penalty could be a death sentence.

The main thing to remember about joining a ship abroad is to BE PREPARED. If possible, always take the following with you:

1) At least one major credit card to cover hotel and/or emergency expenses. (Note that Visa is the world's most widely accepted card.)
2) Enough cash (preferably in the currency of your destination) to cover incidental expenses, and a supply of travellers' cheques (preferably in US dollars, the world's most widely accepted currency) to tide you over until you receive your first wages (which will be at least two weeks).
3) Copies of any appropriate insurance policies (see also the question, 'What if I have an accident or fall ill?').
4) A copy of your contract and/or a letter/fax of offer of employment to show upon request to overseas immigration officials. This particularly applies if you are a non-US citizen entering the United States.
5) The name/address/telephone number of your cruise line and, if

different, your direct employer. And don't forget the name of your ship. This is not as silly as it sounds. Your company may have several vessels, possibly with similar names, in the same dock at the same time, and embarrassing mistakes such as going up the wrong gangway do happen.

6) The name/address/telephone number of the shipping agent used by your cruise line at your port of embarkation, including an 'outside office hours' number. Get this information from your company's head office prior to departure.

7) Your passport and any necessary visas or medical certificates (as mentioned above).

What to Take

The answer to the question of what to pack is a resounding 'as little as possible'. In the same way that tourists usually take too much with them on holiday, so new employees tend to take far too much on their first ship. Just because you're at sea doesn't mean you're on a desert island. You will still have access to pharmacies, supermarkets, boutiques, stationers and department stores in many ports of call and in some cases on the ship itself. So do you really need those six bottles of lotion, 25 music cassettes, mega-size shampoo and conditioner, eleven or twelve T-shirts (you're bound to buy more), umpteen pairs of shoes, outfits you wouldn't even wear at home and your entire library including *War and Peace*?

Your cabin is unlikely to offer even a fraction of the space of your bedroom at home, especially if you have to share it. You will probably spend most of your working time in uniform anyway, and your hours on shore may necessitate little more than a pair of shorts, so be ruthless. Remember too, that crew members usually accumulate additional items on their travels and these may include anything from duty free sound systems to life-size carvings of African giraffes! If your luggage is bursting on the way out, how on earth will you carry it on the way back?

You will, of course, need to choose what to leave in as well as out, and this will depend on:

a) *Your itinerary*. Whether you include sweaters or swimwear will be subject to the general climate of your intended route. If your itinerary is variable, so will your wardrobe need to be varied, but do keep the quantity of each variation to a minimum.

b) *Your job*. Entertainers may need to include costumes; social staff should bring cocktail/formal wear; and most employees will require uniforms.

c) *Your ship*. Different vessels have different dress codes but as a rule of thumb the longer and more expensive the cruise, the glitzier the evening wear and smarter the day wear for social and other non-uniformed staff (see the answer to the question 'What should I wear?' in the section *What to Expect* above).

*Do you really need to pack
your entire library?*

Also, several easy-to-pack items that few first-time crew members consider, but which you may find useful are:

a) *Small hand torch* — in case your cabin or indeed the whole ship is plunged into darkness during a power failure or emergency situation.
b) *Sewing kit* — for speedy repair of hanging hems, lost buttons, etc.
c) *Handful of clothes pegs* — to hang hand-washed items to dry.
d) *Travel alarm clock*
e) *Small padlock* — to secure travel bags and onboard personal effects.
f) *Tube of shoe whitener* (if applicable)
g) *Swiss-style army knife* — or at least a corkscrew/bottle-opener.

When packing, take into account that your luggage could go missing en route to the vessel. Always label your baggage clearly with the name of your ship, your cruise line and the shipping agent in your destination port. If you have more than one item of luggage, split the contents so that you don't have all uniform/formal wear in one case, for example, and all casual/sports wear in the other. The same applies to jewellery, pairs of shoes, underwear, etc. Even if one case goes missing, you will have enough in the other(s) to tide you over until its eventual arrival.

If you intend making a career out of working at sea, it is worth investing in hard, durable cases (such as those by Delsey or Samsonite) which should survive the attentions of even the most frenzied baggage-handler.

THE UNOFFICIAL CHARTS

Just for fun, with all listings in no particular order:

Top Ten Best Bets for General Employment

1. Carnival Cruise Lines
2. Princess Cruises
3. Royal Caribbean Cruise Line
4. Cunard Line
5. Costa Cruise Lines
6. Holland America Line
7. Norwegian Cruise Line
8. Celebrity Cruises
9. P & O Cruises
10. Epirotiki Lines

Top Ten Jobs for Time Off in Port

1. Featured Entertainer
2. Casino Staff Member
3. Gift Shop Assistant
4. Musician
5. Disc Jockey
6. Sports/Fitness Instructor
7. Photographer
8. Cruise Staff Member
9. Cruise Sales Manager
10. Port Lecturer

Top Ten Money Earners

1. Maitre D'
2. Cruise Director
3. Doctor
4. Featured Entertainer
5. Hotel Manager

6. Captain
7. Purser
8. Casino Manager
9. Chief Engineer
10. Food & Beverage Manager

Top Ten Jobs for Perks

1. Cruise Director
2. Hotel Manager
3. Maitre D'
4. Shore Excursions Manager
5. Captain
6. Food & Beverage Manager
7. Doctor
8. Port Lecturer
9. Purser
10. Bars Manager

Top Ten Most Glamorous Jobs

1. Captain
2. Doctor
3. Featured Entertainer
4. Social Hostess
5. Dancer
6. Deck Officer
7. Water Sports Instructor
8. Dance Band Singer
9. Disc Jockey
10. Any Officer with three or more stripes

Top Ten Best Bets for Native English-speaking Jobhunters

1. Gift Shops/Retail
2. Hairdressing/Beauty
3. Shore Excursions
4. Casino
5. Cruise Staff/Entertainment
6. Technical/Engineering
7. Sports/Fitness
8. Hotel Management/Pursers Office
9. Medical
10. Photography

Top Ten Silly Questions from Passengers

1. Does the crew sleep onboard?
2. Do these stairs go up as well as down?

3. Is it sea water in the swimming pool, because it moves around so much?
4. Can we walk ashore when we anchor off?
5. How far are we above sea level?
6. What time is the Midnight Buffet?
7. (To the waiter) Is the fish caught each day by the crew?
8. (To the Captain, at his reception party) Who's driving?
9. (To the featured entertainer) Do you hope to go into Show Business one day?
10. (To anyone who works onboard) So when are you going to get a real job?

Ten Things You Should Know Before Going to Sea

1. You start on ships for the travel, you stay on ships for the money, you end up on ships for ever.
2. Never tell passengers about your favourite shoreside bar, beach or restaurant.
3. The ship's laundry master will insist it is the salt air that has shrunk your best formal wear.
4. The obligatory crew lifeboat drill is always scheduled for your morning off.
5. Attractive females don't need security passes.
6. If travel broadens the mind, working on ships stretches the imagination.
7. Nobody has ever said ship life was fair.
8. Local taxi drivers will always rip you off.
9. If you were sexually unsure at the beginning, you will be totally confused by the end.
10. Cabin walls have ears.

And just for the Ladies . . .

Ten Things Your Mother Never Told You

1. All male crew members are single — even the married ones.
2. The ship's photographer cannot make you a movie star.
3. Neither does the DJ have recording 'contacts'.
4. A leopard doesn't change his stripes.
5. You can't teach an old sea-dog new tricks.
6. An officer is not always a gentleman.
7. Gangways weren't made for stilettos.
8. Never lend your cabin key to the guy who says he's lost his.
9. Buoys will be buoys.
10. Beware of Greek officers bearing gifts.

And everything else your mother told you still applies.

On Deck

Your image of the deck department may include swarthy mariners scaling the rigging or their latter-day counterparts stacking up sun loungers. However the real workings of the Deck Department are rather different. One could say that the members of the deck department are ultimately responsible for getting the ship safely from A to B. They include the navigators on the bridge (always located at the front of the ship), the quartermasters at the wheel, the deckhands chipping and painting the hull, the ABs (Able Seamen) manning the launches to shore, and so on.

Opportunities for Deck Officers

The head of the deck department is also the master of the entire vessel, the *Captain*. He has absolute rights of control over the ship and all those (passengers as well as crew) who sail in her. In other words, what the Captain says, goes. As well as overseeing the navigation, a

Captain's daily routine is largely taken up with paperwork, inspection tours, attending social events and meeting with the various heads of department. Also, international maritime law dictates that only the Captain is allowed to sign verification of the daily entries in the ship's log book, such entries providing an important record of nautical and navigational data, together with reports concerning passengers and crew.

The Captain's assistant is the *Staff Captain* and it is he (rarely she) who is second in command of the vessel. The joke is frequently told that the Staff Captain does all the work and the Captain takes all the glory, and certainly much of the day-to-day running of the ship, together with disciplinary and crew matters, will fall onto the Staff Captain's desk. The Staff Captain will also be a certified Master in his own right and able to take over command at any time, if necessary.

Third in Command is the *Chief Officer,* whose responsibilities include overseeing the maintenance of the body of the ship, i.e. the exterior paintwork, the decks and the hull. He may also arrange for supplies of fresh water and fuel and the disposal of sewerage and garbage, vital services to which most passengers remain oblivious.

The *First Officer* (there are usually several) will spend most of his working hours on the bridge doing watch duty. The bridge is always manned, even in port, and the navigation and safety of the vessel are the responsibility of the officer on duty.

Watch duties on ships always follow the sea-going tradition of four-hourly cycles, i.e. 8am-12 noon, noon-4pm, 4-8pm, 8pm-12 midnight, midnight-4am, and 4-8am. This way, an officer on the 4.00 to 8.00 watch, for example, must be on duty from 4am to 8am and again from 4pm to 8pm, so that his watch hours total eight in every 24.

The job of *Safety Officer* is either held by one of the senior officers alongside their other duties or is a full-time position in its own right. The Safety Officer is responsible for the training and implementing of all safety procedures at sea, including the prevention and combat of fire, possibly the worst hazard on any ship. Note that the master controls for the fire-detection system (including deck plans with indicator lights to locate the problem area) and the watertight doors, which can divide the lower part of the vessel into compartments, are generally located on the bridge.

Training for Deck Cadets

The previously-mentioned posts are all high-ranking positions which bring with them a salary of upwards of $30,000 (£20,000) a year. These are attained only after years of study and practical apprenticeship. For newcomers, the first step to becoming a Deck Officer is to apply directly to the cruise companies (listed at the end of this book) to be taken on as an *Officer Cadet.* Once accepted, the company will pay your salary (starting pay is approximately $150/£100 per week) and sponsor you throughout your training.

Acceptance as an officer cadet usually requires the following from UK applicants:
— aged between 16 and 22 years
— possess at least four GCSEs, including English, Maths and a Science subject, or (for a shortened cadetship) two A-levels
— good health, especially good eyesight (as you will be tested for clear vision without the aid of spectacles or contact lenses).

Most prospective cadets apply during their final year at school, typically in October/November when they are in a position to give their expected exam results, to start training the following November. The average cadetship lasts four years and includes experience both in college and at sea with continual practical and academic assessment. So, presuming you are accepted by a cruise line as an Officer Cadet at the age of 17 and you get through each stage of the course — not to mention all the jobs that no one else wants to do — you could be a Third Officer with a Class III Certificate by age 21.

You would then continue gaining practical experience at sea until, say, the age of 24, when you could go back to college for a year to gain your Class II Certificate and return to sea as a Second Officer.

By the age of 27 and a further two months of intensive college study, resulting in the acquisition of your Class I (Master Mariner) Certificate, known as your Master's Ticket, you might resume work at sea as a First Officer. From then on promotion through the ranks is very much 'dead man's shoes'.

Promotion prospects tend to be slower for Deck Officers on passenger ships than on other vessels like tankers and container ships, mainly because there are numerically far fewer passenger ships than other merchant vessels. Salaries also tend to be lower than in other areas of the shipping industry. But many cruise line officers agree that such disadvantages are outweighed by the social advantages of passenger ships, including access to public rooms and events, the facility to make a wider circle of friends and acquaintances and a generally more glamorous lifestyle.

For those who might like to consider the alternatives, however, high earnings and good promotion prospects are offered on tankers by leading oil companies. But the work is hard, the hours are long and the social life virtually non-existent. Container ships may be seen to be less demanding than tankers but, in terms of prospects and salary, may also be less rewarding, Ferries are the less exotic side of the passenger market, but the routine of returning frequently to a home port may prove attractive to officers with on-shore family or business commitments.

Further details on training and careers for deck officers in the British Merchant Navy may be obtained from the Coordinating Agent, Merchant Navy Officer Training, Carthusian Court, 12 Carthusian St, London EC1M 6EB (tel 0171-702 1100).

Information on specialist courses and career opportunities for Merchant Navy Deck Officers may be obtained from the following colleges:

Clyde Marine, 209 Govan Road, Glasgow G51 1HJ (tel 0141-427 6886). This company has the capacity to place Cadets with shipping companies.

Glasgow College of Nautical Studies, Department of Maritime Studies, 21 Thistle St, Glasgow G5 9XB (tel 0141-429 3201).

Liverpool John Moores University, School of Engineering and Technology Management, Byrom St, Liverpool L3 3AF (tel 0151-231 2294).

Lowestoft College, Maritime & Offshore Centre, St. Peters St, Lowestoft, Suffolk NR32 2NB (tel 01502 583521).

Faculty of Nautical Science, South Tyneside College, St. George's Avenue, South Shields, Tyne & Wear NE34 6ET (tel 0191-427 3500; ext 481).

Maritime Operations Centre, Warsash Campus, Southampton Institute, Newtown Road, Warsash, Hants. SO3 9ZL (tel 01489 576161).

Trinity House, Tower Hill, London EC3N 4DH (tel 0171-480 6601). Awards scholarships/cadetships.

Royal Navy

Finally there's the RN. All the vessels referred to above, including passenger cruise liners, are classed as Merchant ships. The Royal Navy is a totally separate maritime body with distinct ways of operating and training. Although some Merchant officers might have received RN training and may even be in the Royal Navy Reserves, the RN offers a very different and more military career structure.

Anyone wishing to pursue a career with the Royal Navy should contact the Royal Navy & Royal Marines Careers Advice Centre, 151 High St, Southampton, Hampshire (tel 01703 223464).

Finding a Job in the Deck Department

There are agencies which specialise in finding placements for deck officers, engineers and ratings. For addresses, refer to the end of the section *Technical & Engineering Department.*

It is useful to note that cruise lines tend to employ deck officers of the same nationality as the company itself, even if the non-officer staff is multinational. It is therefore important, if only for linguistic reasons, that aspiring deck staff are aware of the nationality bias of prospective companies before applying to join their deck department (this information is provided in the cruise ship listings *Facts About the Ships*). For example Epirotiki Lines uses mainly Greek officers, Costa Cruise Lines employs mostly Italians, American nationals are sought for deck officer positions by American Hawaii Cruises and Clipper Cruise Lines, and Cunard Line hires mainly British officers (although Norwegians have been retained on several of their ships). Possibly the best bet in terms of work opportunities for prospective British deck officers is P & O Cruises (address in *Cruise Lines & Operators* near end of book) as they also have a strong ferry division.

In the Words of a Deck Officer

I'm the junior First Officer onboard a passenger ship in the Mediterranean. There are actually three First Officers on this particular ship and I'm the junior, not because of my age (I'm 31) but because I was promoted to this position more recently than the other two. As the junior, I get the raw deal when it comes to duty times, as I'm on the 12.00 to 4.00 watch. This means I hardly ever get ashore, since I'm always sleeping in the mornings and working in the afternoons, and I can't even enjoy a few drinks in the evening when I know I'm due to start work at midnight. One of the other First Officers is going on leave at the end of next cruise though, and I'll take over his 4.00 to 8.00 watch, which will suit me better.

I suppose of all the jobs on the ship, ours is one of the most insular. During the night there's usually only myself and the quartermaster here on the bridge and even in the daytime I don't have much contact with other employees. Occasionally we'll have bridge visits when I'll explain the workings of the radar and controls to any passengers who might be interested in that sort of thing. But in general, my work is navigation and does not involve the public at all.

Of course, the social side is there if that's what you want. All officers are encouraged to attend the major cocktail parties and the 'Old Man' and 'Staff' both host tables in the passenger restaurant, even though they admit that the small talk can sometimes be an effort. Some deck officers might enjoy that aspect of the job but, for most of us, the organised functions are a bit of a bore and, especially since I've become a Dad, I'm not that bothered about socialising.

My wife (who was a ship's purser before we married) and baby daughter actually spend several weeks a year onboard the ship with me. They may travel free of charge, as long as they occupy my cabin, which is no problem as I have a double bed and a cot can be provided. I am also entitled to about three months paid leave, so I do get to see quite a lot of them.

I must say that although my personal terms of employment are really quite good (they include medical cover and a pension scheme), several of the major cruise lines seem to be introducing contractual changes that will mean less security for deck officers in the future. As for my personal future, who knows? I have my Master's Ticket and eventually it would be good to be based at home working as a harbour pilot, but such jobs are hard to get. If I'm honest, I suppose I would like to be Captain one day, *although on passenger ships it's a slow process. If I were working on cargo vessels I would probably be Master in my own right by now, and earning a lot more than my current $32,000 (£21,300) a year. But in my opinion even the captain of a container ship is underpaid when you consider what a commercial airline pilot can make.*

If money had been my main objective I would definitely have looked to the skies. But like so many of my colleagues I have always loved the sea and love working on the sea. There's nothing quite like the view from the bridge as we're sailing into the sunset or the freedom of seeing ocean for miles on every side. For me, that's what it's all about.

Peter Morton (age 31)

All Hands on Deck

Let's suppose a career as an officer isn't for you and that you're looking for more casual or manual work opportunities within the Deck Department. These include positions as an unskilled *Ordinary Seaman/ Deckhand,* skilled *Able Seaman (AB), Deck Carpenter, Quartermaster* (an AB who assists the deck officers with navigation) and *Bosun* (a senior AB who acts as supervisor and link between the lower ranking seamen and the deck officers, a sort of naval equivalent to a military sergeant).

The fact is your quest for a non-officer position on deck may be frustrating. Openings for deck 'ratings' (non-officers) on passenger ships are extremely limited and, nowadays, companies tend to fill even AB positions with workers from countries with low-wage economies, particularly the Philippines. But if swabbing the deck has always been one of your ambitions, by all means try your luck by writing to the cruise lines direct (see list of *Cruise Lines & Operators*). Try also yacht charterers, cargo ships and ferry companies, as they often have more general opportunities for seamen and might be prepared to sponsor the training.

British applicants fortunate enough to receive sponsorship are normally expected to attend a three-month course, which generally culminates in the Department of Transport Efficient Deck Hand (EDH) examination. In the UK this course is offered at the National Sea Training College, Denton, Gravesend, Kent DA12 2HR (tel 01474 363656).

If the Deck Department doesn't sound quite as promising as you had hoped, never fear. Most newcomers do not find jobs on the bridge, but rather in one of the many departments which combine to turn a cruise ship into a floating hotel. And that's where we'll be looking next.

Hotel Department

The Hotel Department houses by far the most employees on the average cruise ship and therefore offers the most job opportunities to newcomers. It operates in much the same way as a large hotel on land, with various departments (depending on the size of the ship) including food and beverage, restaurants, bars, public rooms and housekeeping, each with their own managers and various assistant managers, all under the overall command of the *Hotel Manager* who is Head of Department. Needless to say, the managerial jobs are senior positions attracting annual salaries from $30,000 (£20,000), and are generally filled by internal promotion. The more basic jobs, by contrast, tend to be paid very badly. On the American model, everyone knows that most of the earnings come from tips.

Some Tips On Tips

There is an old joke amongst cruise line employees that at the end of the voyage the Captain climbs onto his moped and the waiter drives home in his Rolls. While this may be an exaggeration, it is certainly true to say that a high earning potential exists for anyone in the direct service sector (such as waiters, bar waiters, busboys and cabin stewards) providing they are prepared to endure the often long working hours.

*The Captain climbs onto his moped,
the waiter drives home in his Rolls*

Passengers are generally given guidelines on how much they are expected to tip and, although tipping is discretionary, most passengers do follow the company's recommendations. Some passengers may have already pre-paid gratuities at the time of booking, in which case the company will reimburse crew members accordingly. This may not be such a bad thing as the pre-paid service charge is guaranteed and often passengers will tip a little extra as well.

Recent tipping recommendations given to guests by the following cross-section of major cruise lines may serve as a guide to the type of gratuity-making potential to expect, bearing in mind that cabin stewards, waiters and busboys may serve between fifteen and thirty passengers per day. Note that those companies which discourage tipping invariably pay staff a higher basic wage to compensate. Note also that the service charge percentage added to bar bills is generally the same as that added to restaurant wine bills, etc. Figures are given in US dollars, the shipboard currency of most passenger vessels ($1 = approximately 65 pence).

Recommended gratuity rates per passenger per day:

American Hawaii Cruises: $3.50 for cabin steward, $3.50 for waiter, $1.75 for busboy, 15% added to bar bills

Carnival Cruise Lines: $3 for cabin steward, $3 for waiter, $1.50 for busboy, 15% added to bar bills

Celebrity Cruises: $3 for cabin steward, $3 for waiter, $1.50 for busboy, 15% added to bar bills

Clipper Cruise Line: pooled tips of $8 per passenger per day

Club Mediterranée: no tips permitted

Costa Cruise Lines: $3 for cabin steward, $3 for waiter, $1.50 for busboy, $1 for head waiter, 15% added to bar bills

Crystal Cruises: $3.50 for cabin steward, $3.50 for waiter, $2 for busboy, 15% added to bar bills

Cunard Line: $3-$6 for cabin steward and waiter, $1.50-$4 for busboy (both subject to ship), 15% added to bar bills. No tips on *Sea Goddess I and II*

Holland America Line: no tips recommended (although tips may be accepted); no service charge added to bar bills

New Commodore Cruise Line: $3 for cabin steward, $3 for waiter, $2 for busboy, $4 for head waiter, 15% added to bar bills

Norwegian Cruise Line: $3 for cabin steward, $3 for waiter, $1.50 for busboy, 15% added to bar bills

P & O Cruises: $1.50 for cabin steward, $1-$1.50 for waiter (subject to ship), 50 cents for busboy, $1 for restaurant wine steward, 10% added to bar bills

Princess Cruises: $3 for cabin steward, $3 for waiter, $1.75 for busboy, 15% added to bar bills

Radisson Seven Seas Cruises: no tips permitted; no service charge added to bar bills

Royal Caribbean Cruise Line: $3 for cabin steward, $3 for waiter, $1.50 for busboy, 15% added to bar bills

Seabourn Cruise Line: strictly no tips permitted

Windstar Cruises: no tips permitted

Both waiters and stewards tend to agree that shorter cruises are the best (pro rata) for gratuities, while admitting they're harder work. So if making a fast buck is one of your objectives, go for a cruise line that specialises in short party cruises of the 'fun and sun' variety, and you could be laughing all the way to the bank.

But before considering the catering, bar and housekeeping sectors of the hotel department, let us look at office jobs.

PURSER'S OFFICE

One senior manager with a specific shipboard title is the *Purser*. The Purser is chiefly responsible for the ship's accounts, although there are many aspects of the job that fall outside the realm of accountancy, including requisitioning supplies, overseeing printed matter and dealing with customs and immigration officials as well as anyone with a problem. In the days when ships were ships and not floating hotels, the Purser may have also assumed the role that is now allotted to the Hotel Manager. Although a few shipping companies still adhere to the increasingly-outmoded practice of referring to the head of the Hotel Department as the Purser, it is nowadays generally accepted that the Purser's position is different from and subordinate to that of the Hotel Manager.

The Purser (also known as the Chief Purser) may be aided by an *Assistant Purser* or *Hotel Purser* (to oversee all areas of passenger business), a *Berthing Officer* (to allocate accommodation) and various *Second, Third and Fourth Pursers*. Most ships also have at least one *Crew Purser* (and maybe *Assistant Crew Pursers* or *Clerks*) to deal specifically with crew issues and accounts.

Quite often the Purser's office, with its many comings and goings, is seen as the hub of the ship. It is also the perfect place for anyone with secretarial or accountancy skills to offer their services. So if you're interested in typical office work but don't want to work in your typical office, read on. The Purser's office needs *Secretaries* with good typing and basic computer skills. Previous shipboard experience is not essential although ability to work well under pressure is a must. Some temping experience would be an advantage.

The Purser's office also needs qualified *Accountants, Bookkeepers* with experience and/or qualifications, *Office Clerks*, who are eager rather than qualified, and *Receptionists* with basic secretarial skills. Often there is no actual reception area, but the front desk of the Purser's office serves this purpose. Bearing in mind that this is also the place where most passenger complaints are aired, a patient and tactful, not to say thick-skinned, disposition is also beneficial.

In applying for jobs in the Purser's office, an ability to speak at least one foreign language is a definite bonus and, in some cases, might even be a requirement. Experience or qualifications (such as a Higher National Diploma/HND in Hotel Management) would also be advantageous.

Other Office Jobs

Top secretaries are needed as *Personal Assistants* to senior officers. Depending on the size of the ship, the Captain, Chief Engineer and Hotel Manager may all have PAs. Appropriate experience is important for these positions and some specialist technical knowledge may also be desirable. Expect to earn upwards of $20,000 (£13,500) per year.

Other office-based opportunities may include work in a berthing office (allocating cabins), a manifest office (processing embarkations, etc.) or an accommodation office (attending to the servicing of passenger cabins). If this type of work appeals, you should write direct to the Head Office of the respective cruise lines (see *Cruise Lines & Operators* near the end of the book) or to the employment agencies listed at the end of this section (see *Useful Addresses for Jobs in the Hotel Department*).

As with all job applications, the more you can offer, the better your chance of acceptance. Why not enrol on a short course to update your skills (or learn new ones), attend an evening class in computer studies or languages or work for a local temp agency in the meantime?

In the Words of a Fourth Purser

I started work only two months ago as a Fourth Purser onboard a mid-sized ship that normally carries about 800 passengers. I feel that I'm actually quite well suited to this type of work. I have a degree in Business Studies and I also speak reasonable French, two factors that I'm sure helped to clinch the job, even though I never use either. I also have experience in several related areas. I've worked in Greece as a representative for a big holiday company so I'm used to looking after tourists and sorting out their problems. I also did a short spell in a travel agency, where I had to use a computer as well as deal with the public. And I've even sold time-share, which proves I have a sense of humour!

In the winter months the ship sails around Mexico and the Caribbean and in the summer we go up the coast of Alaska. This itinerary means we get a lot of Americans onboard. Being from Scotland, I've had to really concentrate on speaking clearly as, initially, none of the passengers could understand me!

Communication hasn't been my only problem. On my first couple of days I had to enter the list of passenger names (the manifest) into a computer in a small back office. Unfortunately, we had unusually bad weather at the time and I felt really ill. Quite a lot of the passengers were sick too, but that was no consolation. I was literally green, staring at the computer screen in this moving, windowless room while trying to create a good first impression at the same time. In the end, I went to the nurse and she gave me some medication. This cured the sea sickness but made me feel so drowsy that I fell asleep at the keyboard. Some first impression!

My other teething problems concerned clothes or rather the lack of them. As a junior purser, I am a one-stripe officer and wear uniform for work during the day (which I had to buy myself). Longer-serving officers are also expected to keep a more formal uniform (including full-length skirts for the women) to wear at social functions and on particular evenings. As a newcomer, however, I was told I could wear my own clothes if I wished to attend the Captain's Cocktail Party. Since I had assumed I would be in uniform most of the time, I hadn't packed any suitable dresses and had to wear a lycra mini skirt that had seen better days. It certainly got me noticed, but not in the way I would have liked. Neither had I been told that I would also need white or cream shoes for work, which meant I spent my first few hours in Jamaica, searching in vain for a pair of white courts, and ended up using whitener to blanche my favourite sling-backs.

I guess for me it's still early days and I don't know yet if I'll stick it. I hate having to share accommodation with another junior purser, although with promotion I would get a single cabin. I also have bad days working on the front desk when I get sick of hearing passenger complaints. They moan about everything — the noise, the movie schedule, the service, the lack of service, the price of excursions, the price of taxis, the heat, the cold, the weather in general, the air-conditioning, the lack of air-conditioning — and it's even worse on the day before disembarkation, when they're all querying their bills and getting their luggage tags mixed up. On the other hand, I've been to a lot of places I'm sure I would never have visited otherwise and I've made some interesting friends.

Financially, my $1,150 (£760) per month is very much at the lower end of the purser's pay scale, but I find that in spite of spending a lot, I easily save over half my earnings, which is something I would miss if I went back to working onshore. And even though in all honesty I can't see myself doing this in ten years time, the last two months have been a valuable experience that I definitely don't regret and certainly won't forget.

Sarah Knight (age 26)

CATERING FOR ALL

As you might expect in an environment where guests eat around the clock, catering for hundreds of passengers (and crew) is a mammoth task that requires a huge number of staff. The person in charge of all these staff members, plus the administrative planning and budgeting, is the *Food & Beverage Manager* (or F & B Manager). The alternative title *Catering Manager* is preferred on some ships, though the responsibilities are much the same. This important department of the ship also includes the bars under the supervision of a *Bars Manager*.

The F & B Manager will be assisted by various under managers: *Assistant F & B Manager, Junior Assistant F & B Manager* (how about Assistant to the Assistant F & B Manager?), etc. Ships with more than one dining room may also employ a *Restaurants Manager*.

Due to the large numbers of waiting staff required, opportunities may occur more frequently in the restaurants than in any other sector of a cruise ship. Some companies favour European or international personnel and, for this reason, the predominant nationality of restaurant employees on each vessel is included in the *Cruise Ship Listing* later in the book.

If you hold an HND or OND in Hotel Management or Catering Management and have what you consider to be appropriate managerial experience in hotels or restaurants on shore, you might wish to apply for a managerial post at sea which comes with a salary of $25,000 (£16,500) and upwards. Preference will almost always be given to applicants with maritime experience as well as managerial experience. It may be worthwhile accepting a lower-ranking position than you'd prefer in order to get up the gangway as, once onboard, promotion prospects in maritime catering are generally very good.

In the Front Line: Jobs in the Restaurant

Be warned that both restaurant and bar staff work long hours on ships, generally up to 15 hours a day. Much of this time is spent standing around, and stamina is therefore an important prerequisite of the job. It is inadvisable to apply for positions in this department if you are unable or do not wish to live on your feet. Comfortable shoes are a must.

Every restaurant on every ship has its own *Maitre d'Hotel* (maitre d' for short) and often *Assistant Maitre d's* who are in charge of an army of waiters, wine stewards and busboys. The Maitre d' is normally an experienced professional, tactful, possibly a linguist, and with a keen eye to match his earning power of over $45,000 (£30,000) per year including tips.

Waiters should ideally be trained in silver service and have experience in a high class restaurant. Would-be waiters without experience might do better to clinch a job as a *Busboy* (Waiter's Assistant) in the first instance, as promotion prospects for the capable are always bright. Opportunities also exist for inexperienced *Catering Assistants* to clear tables and replenish food supplies in the buffet-style passenger restaurants.

Wine Stewards should possess a good knowledge of wines, obtained by an appropriate college course or work experience. Note that one of the most acclaimed institutions to offer internationally recognised courses of varying lengths and levels is the Wine and Spirit Education Trust, Five Kings House, 1 Queen Street Place, London EC4R 1QS (tel 0171-236-3551).

With the exception of Head Waiters and Head Wine Stewards, basic salaries for wine stewards, waiters and busboys are low, maybe only $50 to $100 (£35 to £65) per week. But with tips and commission, most restaurant staff can easily earn a weekly wage in excess of $500 (£330).

In the Words of a Waiter

I first started working at sea about five years ago when I was 32. My first ship was based in the Mediterranean and used to call at my home port of Istanbul, where at that time I was employed as a waiter in one of the main hotels. A friend who was already working onboard told me they were short of restaurant staff and managed to arrange an interview for me onboard the ship. My work experience, together with the fact that I speak reasonable English, meant I was taken on there and then.

When the company sold that vessel I was offered a job on one of their other ships, sailing out of Florida. I decided to take it even though my wife was unhappy about me working away for nine months at a time, because I knew I would be able to earn more than on land. I have always dreamed of opening my own first-class restaurant in Turkey, and I am not far from realising that goal. Of course, everything has a price and I suppose the price of my dream is not being at home to see my two children grow up. I also miss the home comforts of family life. It comes hard having to share a small cabin with three other waiters and take care of your own cleaning, bed-making and laundry after a ten hour shift in the restaurant.

Yes, we work long hours, sometimes starting at 6.30am, and this includes two sittings for breakfast and dinner or lunch and dinner most days of the week. For this I get a basic salary of $100 (£65) per week. This may sound awful, but my real earnings come from tips. During an average cruise, my busboy and I will serve about 30 passengers each mealtime. These passengers always sit at their allocated table in my section of the restaurant so, by the end of the cruise, I know them quite well. I make a point of remembering the guests' names and chatting with them. Not only does it make the work more enjoyable but they are then more likely to tip well. The ship gives the passengers recommended tipping guidelines of $3 per passenger per day for their waiter and $2 for their busboy. Some guests may tip less but many will tip more. In an average week I clear $630 (£420) in tips and on good cruises I'll do even better. Most of that money I'll send straight home to my wife.

As for expenses, my main expense during this contract has been the cost of my airline ticket to join the ship in Fort Lauderdale, and I'll get that back. Other cruise lines work differently but my particular company always reimburses me for my outward expenses when I've completed each nine-month contract and they also pay for my flight home for my usual two months leave. I supply my own black trousers, white shirts and bow-tie for work, although the company supplies us with uniform jackets.

You do, of course, have to take into account off-the-record 'expenses' such as tipping to get the food quickly in the galley. On my first day at sea I had to wait ages for each course and wondered why other waiters who put their orders in after mine *kept getting their food before me. But I soon discovered that a few well-spent bucks in the galley meant my tables also got their profiteroles pronto.   In some ways, keeping the customer happy is more important at sea than on land because a lot of emphasis tends to be placed on the comment cards which passengers fill in at the end of their cruise. If a waiter gets bad ratings it can result in a demotion to a worse station (section of the restaurant) or a reduction in his number of tables which will of course affect his earning power. Some of the passengers can be demanding but most of them have saved hard to come on their dream cruise and are just out to have a good time. Personally, I enjoy keeping them happy. It's a two-way thing — I help them live their dreams, they help me buy mine.*

Hassan Kaya (age 38)

Behind the Scenes: Jobs in the Kitchen

The standards of cuisine vary of from ship to ship but on the whole are luxurious (see the accompanying sample lunch and dinner menus, typical of a mid-range cruise ship). As in the kitchens of any large hotel, a cruise ship employs numerous chefs under the overall charge of an *Executive Chef* and/or *Head Chef* or *Chef de Cuisine*. Nowadays, these roles are largely administrative and he/she is more likely to be found at a computer than surrounded by steaming saucepans.

The actual food preparation is done by a team of *Sous Chefs, Chefs de Rang, Chefs de Partie, Chefs Entremetier, Sauce Chefs, Pastry Chefs, Commis Chefs* and *Vegetable Chefs*. The team will also include trained *Butchers* and, especially, *Bakers*, as many ships bake their entire bread requirements onboard.

Most vessels offer a self-service option as an alternative to waiter-service at breakfast and lunchtimes, together with a regular late night buffet and an occasional special Gala Buffet. *Buffet Chefs* are, therefore, required to prepare salads and other dishes for these culinary spreads. Rafael Mantas, a buffet chef from the Philippines, explains one of the more unusual aspects of his work:

Alongside my salad-making duties, I carve sculptures out of fruits and vegetables for display in the restaurants. For the Gala Buffets, I also carve featured centrepieces out of huge blocks of ice. I have never had formal training in this art but, like many children in the Philippines, I learnt from an early age how to carve in wood, and the skills required are very similar. Each cruise I give vegetable and ice-carving demonstrations for the passengers and these are usually well attended. I enjoy doing the sculptures as I can carve more or less what I like and it gives me the chance to be creative.

For all senior galley positions, relevant qualifications (such as a City & Guilds Cookery 706 or Baking & Confectionery 120/121) and experience are a must. Indeed, some ships can even boast international chefs who are members of the celebrated *Confrerie de la Chaine des Rotisseurs.* At the upper end of the catering pay scale, top chefs can expect to earn upwards of $35,000 (£23,500) per annum. At the bottom end, a junior vegetable chef may be lucky to make $5,000 (£3,300).

If you are a trained and experienced chef, butcher or baker you should apply direct to the catering department of the cruise lines or to the catering companies listed at the end of this section. Keep your eye too on specialist trade publications such as *The Caterer & Hotel Keeper*, as job vacancies at sea are occasionally, albeit rarely, advertised. The specialist publication, *Rolling Pin International,* which calls itself the 'international hotel and tourism newspaper,' carries some adverts for cruise ship vacancies. Although some job ads are in English, the majority are in German. The magazine can be ordered from PO Box 44, A-8016 Graz, Austria (tel 316-81 12 77).

Courses for *Catering Ratings* (as opposed to senior chefs, who assume officer status) and *Catering Assistants* may be undertaken at the National Sea Training College in Kent (address above in *On Deck*). These courses are all part of sponsorship programmes almost exclusively for merchant shipping companies other than cruise lines which are almost never prepared to fund the training of new recruits.

As opportunities for trainees are so limited, you are strongly advised to obtain an appropriate qualification before applying. Some colleges, notably the Maritime Catering Institute in Salzburg, Austria, even offer special courses in catering at sea.

Positions do exist for unqualified *Galley Assistants* (or is it Slaves?) to do general cleaning and preparation duties, and *Dishwashers* to operate commercial dishwashing machines, but don't apply for either if you are seeking big bucks or job satisfaction. You should be warned that many unskilled jobs on ships offer exploitative salaries, long working hours and poor living standards. Cruise companies assume that most Western Europeans and North Americans will not endure such conditions, and so tend to consider only applicants from developing countries for these types of positions.

Tracey Pardoe, an assistant catering manager from Canada, remarks: *When I joined my first ship I was shocked by the blatant racism onboard. I couldn't believe the discrepancies (monetary and otherwise) between the ranks and the apparent exploitation of sectors of the crew. I've since learned to live with it, but I still can't accept it.*

Frank Kohl, a sous chef from Austria, responds to this comment: *Sure, it's unfair. Life's unfair. But everything's relative. Those guys may work round the clock for a fraction of my earnings, but they can live like kings for that in their country. My salary will barely pay the rent in mine. Some of them have worked at sea for years and no one's making them do it. If they don't like the heat, they can always get out of the kitchen.*

Eduardo Santos, from the Philippines, agrees:

You have to understand that even as a college graduate I can earn more money making sandwiches in the galley than I ever could as a government official in Manila. When you have a young family to support, income is very important.

BEHIND BARS

Most passenger ships have several bars, under the charge of an experienced *Bars Manager* and *Assistant Bars Manager/s*. Many work opportunities exist here for applicants over twenty-one years of age, including jobs for *Cocktail Waiters* to prepare cocktails, *Bar Stewards* to do general bar work and prepare drinks and *Bar Waiters* to take orders, serve drinks and clear tables.

With the exception of managerial positions, which generally assume officer status and minimum monthly salaries of $2,500 (£1,650), earnings in the bar department are often comprised of a basic salary (as low as $50/£35 per week), commission (usually 1.5%) on sales, inclusive service charge (usually 15%) and tips. This can amount to a combined earning potential of at least $2,000 (£1,350) per month, and frequently much more.

For jobs in each category, apply direct to the cruise lines or to the catering companies listed at the end of this section. They will invariably state that experience is essential. But a bit of homework, a good knowledge of cocktails and the ability to bluff can go a long way

In the Words of a Bartender

I live in Miami and have worked in the bar department of a Florida-based ship for the past six months. I first started working at sea on a friend's recommendation. He was already employed as a barman on ships and told me he was saving over $1500 (£1000) a month, going to places he'd never imagined he would actually visit and dating a different girl every cruise. This sounded pretty good to me so I applied to work on the ships too. After writing to loads of different companies and waiting about ten weeks, I was accepted to start the following month.

Of course, one thing my friend forgot to tell me was how long the hours can be. On my first cruise I was so tired I spent my entire free time catching up on my sleep. But after a while I got used to the shifts and now I find it quite easy. I would say to anyone embarking on their first ship to give it at least a month. When you first get onboard, everything's hard because it's all new. You're trying to learn a new job, remember names and faces, find your way around the ship; all this is exhausting enough. It can also be lonely because you're miles from home and you don't know anyone and, because everyone's so busy, it seems no one has time for you. But as you find your feet, you realise this isn't the case and you start making friends and having a laugh. After a few weeks you feel so at home that you can't imagine how you stuck your old routine on land for so long. But you've got to give it time. If you decide on your first day that it's not for you and you disembark at the next port, you've really not given ships — or yourself — a chance.

The other reason for sticking it is that the longer you've been on board, the better your chances of being promoted to the better jobs. For example, I've just been made a bartender which is less hours for the same money as a bar waiter. But, on this ship anyay, you have to start off as a bar waiter. Even though I'd already gained a lot of experience working behind bars on land, including a spell as relief bar manager in a night club, I still had to spend the first few months clearing tables and taking orders. That's just the way it works. There's also a certain amount of luck as to which bar you get allocated to work in, as some are obviously busier than others and this makes a difference to your commission and tips. But we work to a rota, so even if I'm stuck in a quiet bar one week, I'll probably be given a good 'earner' the next.

Surprisingly enough, considering I have a large apartment in Miami, I've even got used to sharing a cabin with two other guys. It's quite cramped but we get on OK and, to be honest, we're hardly ever there at the same time. And as for what my friend said? It's all true, believe me, it's true.

Miguel Lopez

And Don't Forget the Crew

Nearly all cruise ships have separate dining facilities for those who work onboard. The Officer's Mess, Staff Mess and Crew Mess will require chefs, waiters and catering assistants. The Ward Room (i.e. Officers' Bar) and, if applicable, Crew Bar will also need staff. These areas are often a good starting block for personnel with little experience and provide a great opportunity for getting to know fellow crew members. Employees are recruited through the same channels as for passenger areas (see lists of *Catering Concessionaires* below and *Useful Addresses for Jobs in the Hotel Department* at the end of this chapter).

Catering Concessionaires

Many cruise lines do not employ catering and bar staff directly but rather lease the whole concession to a specialist maritime catering organisation. As company policies are subject to frequent change it is advisable to check with their respective head offices before applying as to which catering organisation (if any) they currently use.

Here are some of the main independent agencies and catering companies to the cruising industry:

Carberra NV, Cruise Ship Catering Services (CSCS), 100 South Biscayne Boulevard, Suite 700, Miami, FL 33131, USA. Tel: 305-377-4510.

Also, CSCS, Aigue Marine, 24 Avenue de Fontveille, MC 98000, Monaco. Tel: (3393) 059526.

Innovative Cruise Services, 36 Midlothian Drive, Shawland, Glasgow G41 3QU, Scotland. Tel: 0141-649-8644.

International Services, BP 23, 91250 St. Germain Les Corbeils, France. Tel: 1-60 75 95 95. (French-speaking only)

Logbridge Ltd., South Western House, Canute Road, Southampton SO14 3EW. Tel: 01703 631331. Recruit for Cunard Lines, including the QE2.

Overseas Management, 91 Faubourg St Honoré, F-75370 Paris, Cedex 8, France. Tel: 1-47 06 50 43.

Portfolio International, Greencoats House, Francis St, London SW1P IDH, England. Tel: 0171-834 4499.

Shipping & General UK Ltd, 38 Park St, London W1Y 3PF, England. Tel: 0171-495 1010.

Stellar Maritime Cruise Services, 333 Biscayne Boulevard, Miami, FL 33132, USA. Tel: 305-579-9001. Recruit for Royal Caribbean Cruise Line.

Trident International, 1040 Port Blvd, Suite 400, Dodge Island, Miami, FL 33132, USA. Tel: 305-358-7860.

V Ships, Aigue Marine, 24 Avenue de Fontvieille, PO Box 639, MC 98013, Monaco. Tel: (3393) 051010.

Zerbone Cruise Ship Catering Services, Suite 700, 100 South Biscayne Boulevard, Miami, FL 33131, USA. Tel: 305-374-2491. Recruit for Costa Cruise Lines.

Try also companies like VIP International listed under *Useful Addresses for Jobs in the Hotel Department,* as some also offer specific catering opportunities.

KEEPING THE SHIP SHIP-SHAPE

The housekeeping sector of the Hotel Department is responsible for the general upkeep of the ship's interior and the provision of certain passenger services, under the supervision of the *Chief Steward* and/or *Housekeeper* and *Assistant/s.* Larger ships may also have an administrative centre, under the direction of an *Accommodation Service Manager* (or similar sounding title) to deal with all aspects of maintaining and servicing cabins.

These senior positions with minimum annual salaries of around $25,000 (£16,500) do, of course, require appropriate experience and are often filled by internal promotions. But jobs for the inexperienced newcomer still abound in this division of the ship, so if you can make a bed or mop a floor, read on.

Opportunities in Housekeeping at Sea

No experience? No skills? No matter. *Cleaners* are required for work in all sectors of the Hotel Department, including both passenger and crew areas. The work is often unrewarding and cleaners' salaries are amongst the lowest on the ship (maybe as little as $100/£65 per week). But looking on the bright side, cleaners at sea have little or no overheads (unlike their counterparts on land). And what better place to soak your housemaid's knee than the waters of some balmy tropical shore? Note, however, that cleaning and general maintenance vacancies are often filled by workers from low wage countries. Unskilled Western European or North American job-seekers might do better to apply for other jobs in the Housekeeping Department, such as cabin or pantry steward.

Porters and *Bellmen* may also be required especially on larger ships although many of their typical duties, such as baggage handling on embarkation days, may be undertaken or supplemented by other crew members or shoreside workers. Weekly wages will range between $100 and $150 (£65 and £100) plus tips.

Pantry Stewards are individually responsible for their allocated pantry, one of several small kitchens strategically situated in the passenger accommodation areas. These pantries are often not fully-equipped kitchens, but rather a place for making beverages and snacks. Stewards are expected to keep the pantries clean and take orders for Room Service, which they then prepare and sometimes deliver. Tips can easily treble the low salary (as for porters above).

Cabin Stewards are the maritime equivalent of bedroom stewards in a hotel. Their duties include making beds and general light cleaning, replenishing toiletries and supplies, transferring laundry and delivering food and drinks (Room Service) to their allocated cabins while on duty. They are often supplemented by lower-ranking *Assistant Stewards*, who undertake the collection of cleaning and toiletry supplies for an entire section of cabins from the ship's stores, together with tasks such as furniture removal and deep-cleaning of carpets and upholstery. The basic salary is subject to the number of occupied cabins (up to twenty doubles) in a steward's charge each cruise, but may be as low as $300 (£200) per month. This is not as dire as it sound since it is possible for them to make more than $2,000 (£1,350) per month in gratuities.

Note that cleaners, cabin stewards and sometimes even restaurant staff may be expected to assist as porters and baggage handlers at times of embarkation and disembarkation. Cleaners, baggage handlers, porters and pantry stewards may also be required to work night shifts.

On-the-spot job opportunities are most frequently found in the cabin servicing as well as catering sectors of the ship. These departments can provide a great way in, as in the case of Sylvia Vujinovic from Croatia:

I took a job as a cabin stewardess because I could not get work as a qualified teacher in my home country and I needed to earn some reasonable money. I had been at sea about five months when the position of Purser's Clerk was advertised internally. I asked to be considered and was offered the job. Although I actually earn less now than I did as a stewardess, the work is more interesting and the promotion prospects are excellent. In time, I could even end up as Chief Purser.

In the Words of a Cabin Steward

I work as a Cabin Steward on a ship that often calls in Jamaica where I come from, so I get to go home quite often. I first got hired through a friend of a friend (it always helps if you know someone who's already working on a ship). I've been at sea for three years now, so I guess I must enjoy the lifestyle.

My daily hours are from 9am till 1pm and from 5pm till 9pm, although I often have collection or preparation duties outside of these times. These hours actually suit me fine, as I always have time after lunch in the mess to go ashore or take a nap. After 9pm I usually work out in the crew gym before meeting the guys in the crew bar. I'm also a member of the ship's soccer team and about once a week we'll arrange to play against some local club or other. When I'm not lifting weights or (hopefully!) scoring goals, my job helps to keep me fit. As any housewife will tell you, cleaning and making beds, especially if it's 25 a day, is physical work. When I first come back from vacation I always get tired, but you soon get geared up to it again. It's what you get used to.

We each have our own station of between 11 and 16 cabins and on my ship these are allocated by the Chief Steward. Of course, some stations are better than others and everyone wants the most number of passengers for the tips. Usually, the more experienced stewards get the best deal, but we change stations every other cruise, so even newcomers can get a good section once in a while. Naturally, we all prefer it when the ship is full. On a good week, I can make $800 (£530) in tips alone, that is if I have 15 occupied cabins, with maybe 12 of them doubles, and the tips average the company's recommended $3 a day. Of course, if half my cabins are empty and two of them have single occupancy, I may only make $300 (£200). I suppose on average I earn about $550 (£360) in weekly tips, most of which I manage to save as I have no onboard expenses.

Apart from servicing the cabins and making the beds, I also take the towels and sheets and any garments the passengers want to be cleaned down to the laundry. Then, during my early evening shift, I deliver the next day's programmes, turn down the bedding and do my 'Tooth Fairy' routine of leaving a chocolate on each pillow.

Passengers can order Room Service around the clock, and if it's during my hours I'll deliver it to them. Outside my hours, the duty pantry assistant delivers the orders. It's like this: I work hard when I'm on duty, but when I'm off duty, I don't even think about the job. When I'm off, my time's my own.

Winston Edwards

USEFUL ADDRESSES FOR JOBS IN THE HOTEL DEPART-MENT

In addition to the previously-listed catering concessionaires, the following agencies offer both catering and general employment opportunities in the Hotel Departments of cruise ships, including positions for pursers and secretarial staff, housekeepers, cabin stewards/esses, bar staff and restaurant personnel:

Apollo Ship Chandlers, 1775 NW 70 Avenue, Miami, FL 33126, USA. Tel: 305-592-8790. Recruit for Chandris Cruises, among others.

BlueSeas International Cruise Services Inc, 122 West 26th St, Suite 1202, New York, NY 10001. Tel: 212-255-3326. Vacancies registered in the deck and engine departments, hotel, galley, salon and gift shops. Their new International Seafarers' Exchange undertakes to match cruise ship vacancies with qualified staff who pay a membership fee starting at $300.

Büro Metro, PO Box 626, CH-8039 Zürich, Switzerland. Tel: 1-201 4110. Registration fee of SFr30.

CTI Recruitment & Placement Agency Inc, 1439 SE 17th St, The South Port Center, Fort Lauderdale, FL 33316-1709, USA. Tel: 305-728-9975.

Columbia Ship Management (CSM), Crew Service Ltd, Columbia House, Dodekanison St (PO Box 1624), Limassol, Cyprus. Tel: 5-320900. Recruit for Cunard Line.

Cruise Line Appointments, 142 Parkwood Road, Bournemouth BH5 2BW. Tel: 01202 433464.

Global Ships Services Inc, 141 NE Avenue, Suite 203, Miami, FL 33132, USA. Tel: 305-374-8649.

Greyhound Leisure, 8052 NW 14th St, Miami, FL 33126, USA. Tel: 305-592-6460.

International Cruise Management Agency, Jernbanetorget 4B, N-0154 Oslo, Norway. Tel: 22-33-49-30. Recruits for a range of companies including Crystal Cruises.

Lawson Marine Services Ltd, Royale House, 2 Palmyra Place, Newport, Gwent NP9 4EJ, Wales. Tel: 01633 257558. Experienced management personnel only for hotels, bars and as pursers.

Marine and Mercantile Enterprises, Inc, 6925 Biscayne Boulevard, Miami, FL 33138, USA. Tel: 305-759-5900.

Maritime Management Services Ltd (MMSL), Kristen 20, A-6094 Axams, Austria. Tel: 5234 5230. Recruit for Costa, Norwegian Cruise Line, etc.

Poseidon Services, 1007 North America Way, Miami, FL 33132, USA. Tel: 305-634-3444.

Quest Appointments Ltd, Binning House, 4-6 High St, Eastleigh, Hampshire SO50 5LA. Tel: 01703 644933. Recruit for Princess Cruises, ferry companies, etc.

RG International, 7 Buckland Road, Maidstone, Kent. Tel: 01732 874876.

Seachest Associates, c/o Carnival Cruise Lines, 3655 NW 87th Avenue, Miami, FL 33178, USA. Tel: 305-599-2600. Recruit exclusively for Carnival Cruise Lines.

Supersearch International Ltd, Suite 8, 1 Pink Lane, Newcastle upon Tyne NE1 5DW. Tel: 0191-233-0404.

Travelmate, 52 York Place, Bournemouth BH7 6JN. Tel: 01202 431520.

VIP International, 17 Charing Cross Road, London WC2H 0EP. Tel: 0171-930 0541. Recruit for Holland America Line, Windstar Cruises, etc.

Other Unusual Jobs at Sea

A huge variety of other kinds of work are subsumed by the Hotel Department. Note that Baggage and Laundry Masters, Stores Managers and most Security Personnel (described below) normally rank as Petty Officers, a rank midway between officer and crew member. Other Petty Officer positions might include Medical Orderlies/Dispensers and Assistant Housekeepers. On this subject, however, it should be noted that the status and salary attached to a particular job can vary enormously from company to company and even between ships within the same company. So if you're not happy with the deal you're offered, do shop around.

IN THE HOTEL DEPARTMENT

Baggage Masters supervise the handling and storage of suitcases, trunks and other items. On smaller ships this may be undertaken by staff from the the Purser's Office, whereas larger ships employ specific personnel for this responsibiity. The salary is generally about $1,000 (£650) a month.

Stores Managers are needed to deal with the ordering, logging and storing of all provisions and supplies. This has become an increasingly administrative position, requiring appropriate skills. But larger ships may have openings for untrained *Stores Assistants* to help with the more manual aspects of the job. Earnings for managers and assistants may be approximately $2,000 (£1,350) and $1,000 (£675) respectively per month.

Garbage Handlers assist with the collection and disposal of the mountains of rubbish luxury cruises generate. Cruise ships are notorious for waste and the garbage handlers have an unenviable task. While food and other degradable waste can be legally dumped at sea, specialist garbage barges in ports assist with the removal of additional trash (although some shipping lines have been guilty, inexcusably, of dumping non-degradable waste such as plastics into the oceans). Training and experience are not required but earnings are low (approximately $100/£65 per week) and positions tend to be monopolised by workers from low-economy countries.

Concierges are employed to attend to specific passenger needs, such as arranging tickets and transportation, making onshore theatre or hotel reservations and acting as a general liaison. This position does not exist on all ships, but is confined to the more exclusive luxury vessels. Good organisational skills and a tactful manner are important assets and previous experience in public relations would definitely be useful. Average earnings here may range from $1,500 to $2,500 (£1,000 to £1,650) and upwards per month.

Carpenters and Joiners do far more than carpentry and joinery. In fact, the Hotel Carpenter/Joiner is often more of a general Handyman who must be able to do anything from make a new notice-board to repair a damaged chair. Obviously, relevant qualifications, such as a City & Guilds Certificate, would be advantageous. Be warned, however, that many ships have a tendency to fill such positions with workers from countries such as the Philippines or Indonesia, and for salaries as low as $100 (£65) per week.

Security Officers enforce security procedures on ships and are answerable to a *Chief Security Officer*. These are responsible positions covering all aspects of security from issuing and checking identity papers to enforcing fire and safety regulations and carrying out regular clock patrols. In keeping with modern anti-terrorist techniques, the Chief Security Officer on high-profile ships may even be from a military background and fully trained in bomb disposal. Security may be a potential area for mature applicants with an appropriate career background.

Candidates with British naval experience or (especially) ex-Marines might do well to contact a company which supplies security personnel to various cruise lines, including Crystal Cruises: International Maritime Securities, The Garden House, Little Chilmington, Great Chart, Ashford, Kent TN23 3DN (tel 01233 643805).

Applicants with British police (or similar) experience may have more success with Logbridge Ltd, an affiliation of Cunard Line (see *Catering Concessionaires* above for the address).

Security Officers earn anything between $600 and $3,500 (£400 and £2,350) per month, subject to status, service and (it has to be said) nationality.

Laundry Masters are required to supervise the handling of all the ship's laundry. Considering the huge amount of cleaning involved, including officer and crew uniforms, passenger clothes, evening dresses, upholstery, tablecloths and napkins, bedlinen, etc., the task is enormous. It is not surprising then that the Laundry Master is aided by numerous *Laundry Assistants*. What may be surprising is the difficulty newcomers experience in landing a job in this field, for two reasons. In the first place, candidates need to be familiar with the machinery and cleaning techniques involved in commercial laundry work. Secondly, in keeping with seafaring tradition, many ships employ only laundry workers of Chinese origin. For most of these employees, the laundry, situated deep in the bowels of the ship, is not merely a workplace but an eating place (and often where they cook their own choice of food) and place of relaxation. Chinese videos may be playing on the TV, and Cantonese may be the only language spoken. In other words, the laundry is a self-contained community, more than any other section of the ship. So unless you happen to be from an appropriate cultural background, you might as well forget the idea of becoming a laundry assistant.

Medium to large-sized vessels may also require an *Upholsterer* and/or a *Tailor,* with proven practical ability in these areas. But salaries tend to be low and again oriental workers are frequently hired for such positions.

ELSEWHERE ON BOARD

While you may already be aware of the more obvious job categories discussed above, work opportunities exist in areas that you may not even have considered. For example, did you know that there is so much greenery on the *Sun Princess* that the ship carries a full-time gardener? Or that the *QE2* has its own onboard florists to cope with its huge floral requirements and trained kennel staff to care for passengers' pets and two full-time professional librarians in charge of its books? (The latter are supplied by the maritime library concessionaire, Ocean Books of 15 Beaumont Business Centre, Beaumont Close, Banbury, Oxon. OX16 7TN; 01295 266631.)

Admittedly, such positions are rare, since animals are generally disallowed and most ships' libraries and pot plants are attended by members of the cruise staff or crew. But they do exist, as do the following categories of work.

Computer Technicians are in increasing demand, often to work throughout a company's fleet, modifying data and educating shipboard personnel. Appropriate experience and/or qualifications and the ability to work unsupervised and under pressure are essential requirements, but annual earnings can exceed $60,000 (£40,000).

Printers are needed on many vessels, and very large ships may have a well-equipped print room employing half a dozen staff members. They are responsible for churning out hundreds or even thousands of daily programmes (giving updated information on entertainment, activities, opening times, etc.), world news sheets, menus, party invitations, letterheads, printed cards and more. Smaller ships may offload much of their requirements to shoreside printers, leaving little more than the daily programme and news sheets to be done by a single onboard employee. But there are enough larger vessels afloat to allow reasonable work opportunities for suitably qualified and experienced applicants. Expect to earn about $1,400 (£950) a month.

Journalists may be required, especially on larger ships, to compile the daily programme/news sheet. This can be a rewarding job, with an annual earning potential of $14,000 (£9,500) for self-motivated individuals with flair and experience.

Butlers may be required on ships at the more luxurious end of the market where passengers in certain suite rooms receive the services of a private butler. Appropriate training and/or experience is essential for such work. Job openings here tend to be limited, however, largely because existing butlers often retain their position for years. Although the nature of the job allows little free time, gratuities are generally excellent, often exceeding $800 (£550) per week.

Port Lecturers

As the name implies, the *Port Lecturer* is employed to give talks, slide shows and, especially, shopping information on the various ports of call. Although he/she may work closely with the excursion office staff and Cruise Director (even doing a job often associated with the Cruise Director), the Port Lecturer is frequently under contract to an independent company and may make substantial commission, subject to the allocated ship and itinerary, potentially in excess of $1,000 (£650) per week. Bonuses are paid by retail outlets in popular shopping ports for recommending particular outlets. Note, however, that as payment is generally on a commission-only basis, the reverse side of the coin is that it is also possible to make nothing at all. Some experience of the retail sector, a good background knowledge of the respective ports of call and the ability to bluff when the questions get tough is a definite bonus.

The following companies specialise in supplying Port Lecturers to cruise ships:

On Board Promotions Group, 777 Arthur Godfrey Boulevard, Suite 320, Miami Beach, FL 33140, USA. Tel: 305-673-0400.

Panoff Publishing Inc, 10 Fairway Drive, Suite 200, Deerfield Beach, FL 33441, USA. Tel: 305-426-0046.

International Voyager Media, 11900 Biscayne Boulevard, Suite 300, Miami, FL 33181, USA. Tel: 305-892-6644.

An increasingly popular off-shoot of port lecturing is the unlikely-sounding cruise job of *Art Auctioneer* which consists of selling prints of works of art on the ships themselves. Art auctioneers with a strong background in retail are generally recruited through the same channels as port lecturers, with equally variable commission-earning potential.

Another sales job with a difference is that of *Cruise Sales Manager.* Employed directly by the cruise line, he/she is responsible for booking advance cruises (often with generous incentives) to regular passengers while they are still enjoying the current one. A basic salary of $300 (£200) and upwards per week may easily be doubled by commission for preaching to the converted.

And talking of preaching, a job that is rarely thought of but often exists on bigger ships and longer cruises is that of *Priest* or minister of religion. Although religious services may be conducted by the Captain, many large ships will have an onboard chapel or even a synagogue, together with a resident priest or rabbi, who is there as much for the benefit of the crew as for the passengers. These positions may be of a short-term unsalaried nature (a sort of all-expenses-paid working holiday) or, occasionally, as an actual paid member of the ship's company. Terms and conditions for clerics, as for medics (see *Medical Department*), vary enormously from ship to ship. But an interesting lifestyle may be enjoyed by suitably qualified theologians who 'have cassock, will travel'!

Couriers

If you have previous experience of the travel industry or public relations, are sociable, responsible and have good organisational skills, then you might wish to consider applying to independent tour operators and travel organisations to be a *Group Escort* or courier on their cruise ship holidays. Many travel companies employ individuals (and sometimes couples) to escort their passengers on cruises. Conditions vary: some companies pay very respectable salaries to their group escorts and others offer little more than a subsidised holiday. But all escorts are normally entitled to full passenger status, together with perks such as free shore excursions.

Naturally, companies paying a professional wage will expect a professional level of service, which may include organising cocktail parties, providing information, manning a hospitality desk and being generally available. This type of work is particularly suited to mature people who are usually (though not invariably) women who prefer intermittent employment to a full-time working commitment. If this is you, write direct to independent travel companies that offer cruise holidays, not the cruise lines themselves. Companies include:

Grand Circle Travel, 347 Congress St, Boston, MA 02210, USA. Tel: 617-350-7500.

Page & Moy Ltd, c/o Cruise Product Manager, 136-141 London Road, Leicester LE2 1EN. Tel: 01942 526121.

Princess Tours, 2185 2nd Avenue, Suite 400, Seattle, Washington 98121-1299, USA. Tel: 206-728-4207. Affiliated to Princess Cruises. Mainly summer season work in Alaska.

SAGA Holidays, The Saga Building, Middleburgh Square, Folkestone, Kent CT20 1AZ. Tel: 01303 711523.

Vantage Travel Service, Inc, Corporate Headquarters, 111 Cypress St, Brookline, MA 02146, USA. Tel: 617-734-8000.

Westours, 300 Elliott Avenue West, Seattle, Washington 98119, USA. Tel: 206-281-3535. Affiliated to Holland America Line. Also provides shore excursion personnel for the Holland America fleet.

Of course, *Travel Agents* and *Cruise Consultants* with tour operators frequently get discounted holidays or free 'working trips' (i.e. escorting clients) on cruise ships. For those who enjoy the lifestyle but don't necessarily want the full-time commitment of an on-board contract, working for a travel agency could provide the answer. Request the list of member agencies from the UK organisation PSARA (Passenger Shipping Association of Retail Agents, 9-10 Market Place, London W1N 7AG; tel 0171-436 2449) or from Cruise Lines International Association in the United States (500 Fifth Avenue, Suite 1407, New York, NY 10110).

Opportunities for Bankers

Anyone who currently works in a bank or foreign exchange and wants to work in a similar capacity at sea will be pleased to learn that there are opportunities for bankers. Interested candidates may wish to apply to the Personnel Department of Travelex Financial Services Ltd (65 Kingsway, London WC2 6TD; tel 0171-405 7206). Travelex is the major banking concessionaire on cruise ships worldwide. Although previous relevant experience is a general requirement for work on ships, Travelex also have concessions in other areas of the travel industry, such as airports, where there are more opportunities for inexperienced newcomers to get a foot in the door.

In the Words of a Cashier

I work as a bank cashier onboard a mid-sized cruise ship in the Mediterranean. The Med offers more opportunities for cashiers than most other itineraries because we provide a Bureau de Change. Although the US dollar is internationally accepted, passengers in Europe still need various currencies.

Although I had little experience of dealing in foreign exchange when I joined my first ship, I had worked as a cashier for a major bank in London, and I'm sure that gave me the edge when I applied to work at sea. Initially, I was on a bigger ship with two other cashiers, but now I work alone.

I enjoy my job because, in spite of working closely with the Purser's office, I am basically my own boss and one of the few people on the ship to work relatively normal hours. Of course, I sometimes end up working late, especially towards the end of the cruise, when accounts are being settled and figures printed out. But, in general, I'm free in the evenings to do as I please.

Occasionally that means a drink in the officers' bar (I'm a one and a half stripe officer) or the public rooms, but usually I just like to relax in my cabin. Like a lot of employees onboard, I hire movies from video shops in our regular ports of call or from the crew bar, which has a small video library. My boyfriend, the stores manager, often joins me for a quiet night in with a good movie, a few beers and an extra large bag of popcorn. So it's just like being at home really.

Alison Fitzpatrick (age 29)

Entertainment

The entertainment division of the hotel department is one of the most diverse, incorporating singers, cabaret dancers, DJs, musicians of all kinds, guest lecturers and specialist experts, hosts and hostesses, stage and TV technicians, fitness and sports instructors, children's counsellors, and so on. The people in charge of organising the social programme are called *Cruise Staff*.

On land, the head of such a department would probably assume the title of Entertainments Manager or head of the Social & Entertainment Department. At sea, he/she is known as the *Cruise Director* (commonly abbreviated to CD). By tradition, Cruise Directors come from an entertainment background and may even be a featured act or entertainer in their own right. They are generally very experienced in the maritime leisure industry and assume a high profile position on the ship, compering shows, organising events, giving port lectures and information. Although their role is becoming increasingly administrative and many of the perks of the job are less in evidence, the position of Cruise Director can still offer a very attractive lifestyle and salary (sometimes in excess of $70,000/£46,000 per year) to those with the appropriate skills, aptitude and experience.

Cruise Staff

The Cruise Staff sector of the ship provides some of the most interesting work on a ship. Anyone with an outgoing nature who enjoys the social side of life may well find their niche here. An ability to entertain is a distinct advantage and some companies require cruise staff members to have the capacity to perform in shows or do a featured act. For this reason, people with a theatrical background are attracted to this type of work. Fluency in foreign languages is also advantageous and will almost certainly give you an edge over other applicants. But the main requirements are personality, versatility and the ability to keep smiling even on a cold gangway at 7 o'clock in the morning.

If you wish to apply to join the Cruise Staff in any of the varied capacities outlined below, you should contact the Head of Entertainment at the head office of the respective cruise lines or try one of the agencies listed under *Addresses of Cruise Staff Employers* later in this section.

Note that in the United States, competition for cruise staff work is so intense that two ex-cruise directors of Royal Caribbean Cruise Line have formed an institute to provide courses for aspiring social/entertainment staff. The Cruise Career Training Institute is based at 729 SE 17th St, Fort Lauderdale, FL 33316 (tel 305-561-7327).

Depending on the size of the ship, the Cruise Staff will include some or all of the following members. The *Deputy Cruise Director* or *Assistant Cruise Director* is the CD's right hand man/woman, sharing the workload of programming events and overseeing the smooth running of the department. Traditionally, this is a responsible position, with a general earning capacity of between $2,500 and $4,000 (£1,650 and £2,650) per month. But the title is frequently abused by certain cruise lines, who bestow it upon almost anyone in the social sector, irrespective of ability and experience.

Some ships may also employ a *Social Director* (with comparable earning potential to the Assistant CD) to assist with specific areas such as organising duty rotas and the working schedules of the Gentlemen Hosts (described later). The *Social Hostess* (or *Social Directress*) has potentially the most glamorous job on the ship. At the forefront of the social scene, she is the one making sure all those parties go with a swing. She will direct many of the onboard activities and one of her tasks may be to greet and introduce hundreds of passengers to the Captain at each welcoming cocktail reception. Monthly income here may vary between $2,000 and $3,500 (£1,350 and £2,350).

The position of Social Hostess is possibly the only job on the ship which is invariably allocated to a woman. Females are generally under-represented in most departments but have the greatest opportunities in the hotel division, especially the entertainment/social department where they are slowly breaking through into top positions.

Larger ships may have several Hostesses, all participating in general cruise staff duties and possibly incorporating individual specialities such as childcare or language skills. Depending on the cruise, the number of hostesses employed and the status given to the job, earnings may range between $850 and $3,000 (£560 and £2,000) per month. It is very rare for hostesses or any member of the cruise staff to receive tips but there are often privileges and perks (such as drinks allowances) attached to this type of work.

If you are fluent in at least one language other than English, and preferably more, you may wish to apply your skills as an *International Host(ess)*, for similar earnings to the above. In this capacity you would translate information such as menus and daily programmes, make appropriate broadcasts and announcements, escort tours and generally assist the non-English speaking passengers onboard. Even if you do not wish to specialise in this way, linguistic ability is always needed on ships, so don't forget to mention any languages you speak and to what level when you apply.

If you have secretarial/computer skills and the desire to work your way for $1,000 (£650) and upwards per month, you may also like to consider a very specialised type of job in the cruise staff sector, that of *Programme Coordinator.* The main responsibility of the Programme Coordinator is to lay out the format for the ship's daily programme on computer prior to its being printed. If you are good at English and with an artistic flair this position could be for you, particularly if you enjoy working behind the scenes. Unlike most other jobs in the department, the Programme Coordinator is office-based and may even be required to double up as secretary to the Cruise Director. Sometimes the Daily Programme will take on more of a newspaper format, in which case a journalistic background may be a requirement (see earlier section *Unusual Jobs at Sea*).

Childcare Positions

Children's Counsellors and *Youth Counsellors* (together with *Nursery Assistants* and/or *Nannies*) are often required, especially on larger ships where there may be a separate programme of children's events. It is normally the counsellors who are directly responsible for devising the programme of activities, in conjunction with the Cruise Director. These cater to different age groups, for example two to four, five to eight, nine to 13, and older teenagers 14 to 19.

Appropriate qualifications (such as the widely recognised NNEB nanny diploma) and/or training in child education or child psychology will certainly lend weight to an application, but a genuine interest in working with children or teenagers is the vital key to success in this field. Companies such as Premier Cruise Lines, Carnival Cruise Lines, a Singapore-based company called Star Cruise and, especially, the new

SAMPLE DAILY PROGRAMME OF CHILDREN'S ACTIVITIES

TODDLERS CLUB (Ages 2 - 4)

10.00am - 10.30am	Fun with Balloons	Playroom
10.30am - 11.00am	Let's Colour it in!	Playroom
11.00am - 11.30am	Making Handprints	Playroom
11.30am - 12noon	Let's Learn our ABC!	Playroom
2.00pm - 2.30pm	Fun with Bricks	Playroom
2.30pm - 3.00pm	Nursery Rhymes with Bobby Bear	Playroom
3.00pm - 3.30pm	It's Cartoon Time!	Playroom
5.00pm - 6.00pm	Let's Jump in the Fun Pit!	Playroom
7.00pm - 8.00pm	It's Video Time!	Playroom
8.00pm - 9.00pm	Teddy Bears Party - Bring a Furry Friend!	Playroom
9.00pm - 9.30pm	Storytime	Playroom
9.30pm	Babysitting Begins (Parents, please sign up before 5.00pm)	Playroom

JUNIOR CRUISERS (Ages 5 - 8)

10.00am - 11.00am	Let's Make a Mobile!	Playroom
11.00am - 11.30am	Potato Prints	Playroom
11.30am - 12noon	Buttons, Badges and Brooches	Playroom
2.00pm - 2.30pm	Bingo! Win Fun Prizes!	Playroom
2.30pm - 3.00pm	Start Making Your Shell Box	Playroom
3.00pm - 3.30pm	It's Cartoon Time!	Playroom
5.00pm - 6.00pm	Find the Pirate's Treasure!	Playroom
7.00pm - 8.00pm	It's Video Time!	Playroom
8.00pm - 9.00pm	Indoor Beach Party (wear your beach gear)	Mega-disco
9.00pm - 9.30pm	Let's Limbo!	Mega-disco
9.30pm	Juniorsitting Begins (Parents, please sign up before 5.00pm)	Playroom

CADET CLUB (Ages 9 - 13)

10.00am - 10.30am	Early Bird Bingo	Teen Club
10.30am - 11.30am	Make a Puppet Pirate!	Teen Club
11.30am - 12noon	Let's Write a Puppet Show!	Teen Club
2.00pm - 2.30pm	Crazy Word Search. Whoever finds the most words wins the prize!	Teen Club
2.30pm - 3.00pm	Tell Us A Joke!	Teen Club
3.00pm - 3.30pm	Round-the-Ship Scavenger Hunt	Teen Club
5.00pm - 6.00pm	Kite Flying	Lido Deck
7.00pm - 9.30pm	Let's Watch a Movie!	Teen Club
9.30pm	Cadetsitting Begins (Parents, please sign up before 5.00pm)	Playroom

TEEN CLUB (Ages 14 - 17)

10.00am - 10.30am	Ping Pong Tournament	Sports Deck
10.30am - 11.00am	Shuffleboard Tournament	Sports deck
11.00am - 12noon	Splash Out at our Pool Games!	Poolside
2.00pm - 3.00pm	2nd Round of our Scrabble Tournament	Teen Club
3.00pm - 3.30pm	Quiz! Quiz! Quiz!	Teen Club
3.30pm - 5.00pm	See you at the Pool!	Poolside
5.00pm - 6.00pm	The Dating Game - Team Fun!	Teen Club
7.00pm - 9.30pm	Let's Watch a Movie!	Teen Club
9.30pm - 10.00pm	'Name That Tune' - Chart Quiz	Mega-disco
10.00pm - 11.00pm	Pig-out on Pizza Party!	Mega-disco
11.00pm - 12 midnight	Teens-only Disco	Mega-disco

Disney Cruise Lines may have more openings in this sector than most since they specialise in the family market. Approximate monthly salaries of $850 (£560) and upwards are paid, subject to the age and experience of the applicant.

Sports and Fitness Instructors

Frequent opportunities arise for *Fitness Instructors, Water Sports Instructors* and *Sports Directors* to work in the cruise staff department (as distinct from the spa/gymnasium concessionaires, described later in *Spas and Fitness Centres*). It should be pointed out that the standard is generally high and applicants should be suitably qualified and experienced in coordinating fitness programmes, aerobics classes and/or specialist activities). Expect to earn about $1,500 (£1,000) and upwards per month.

Water Sports Instructors should be qualified dive instructors preferably with qualifications from two internationally recognised examining bodies, principally PADI (Professional Association of Diving Instructors) or SSI (Scuba Schools International). Additional experience and qualifications in related areas such as water-skiing, jet-skiing, Zodiac-driving and parasailing are advantageous. Instructors are usually also responsible for the maintenance of scuba and other equipment.

The smaller (and often upmarket) vessels of companies such as Club Méditerranée, Star Clippers, Windstar Cruises and Cunard Line's *Sea Goddesses* are particularly worth a try for Water Sports Instructors, together with the bigger ships of Princess Cruises, Royal Caribbean Cruise Line (RCCL) and Norwegian Cruise Line (NCL). NCL also operates extensive 'Sports Afloat' theme cruises, featuring specialist celebrity speakers.

Technical Assistants

Most medium-sized ships will have a *Stage Manager* to take care of all the technical aspects of the entertainment programme, from setting up microphones for visiting lecturers to handling the sound and lighting requirements of sophisticated production shows. Larger ships may employ several *Stage Technicians* for this purpose, including specific *Sound and Lighting Engineers*. If the ship has its own onboard TV station, as the bigger ships do, there are even opportunities for a *Television Station Manager* to take charge of broadcasting its extensive programme of videos, satellite TV and other programmes, including regular in-house interviews and features filmed onboard the ship. Appropriate qualifications and experience are a general requirement for all jobs of this nature, with earning potential in excess of $3,000 (£2,000) per month.

There are also job opportunities for general Cruise Staff Members, who may be viewed as the maritime equivalent of Red Coats/Blue Coats/ *animateurs*. They have a high profile onboard, assisting with the many games, activities and scheduled events, embarkation/disembarkation and escorting the organised tours. Salaries vary considerably and are subject to age and experience, but $1,000 to $2,500 (£650 to £1,650) per month should serve as a guide.

Addresses of Cruise Staff Employers

As well as applying directly to the Head of Entertainment at cruise lines, try also the following agencies:

Blue Seas International Cruise Services Inc, 122 West 26th St, Suite 1202, New York, NY 10001. Tel: 212-255-3326. A consultation fee and commission is payable.

Ellen Butterworth Associates, 31 Park Rise, Dawlish, Devon EX7 9RT. Tel: 01626 888264.

Floating Fleet Ltd, PO Box 4216, Portland, ME 04101, USA. Tel: 207-772-7457.

Ship Services International, Inc, 370 West Camino Gardens Boulevard, Third Floor, Boca Raton, FL 33432, USA. Tel: 407-391-5500. Application processing fee from $25.

In the Words of a Social Hostess

Although I am currently working as the Social Hostess on a passenger ship cruising in the Baltic Sea, I am frequently transferred to other vessels within the fleet. I quite enjoy moving around since you meet more people that way and discover new itineraries. Interestingly enough, my job also differs quite a lot from ship to ship, so flexibility is important. During a typical day at sea, I might be expected to host a get-together for single passengers, organise a general knowledge tournament, give a scarf-tying demonstration, narrate a cookery demonstration, attend several cocktail parties, and be generally on the go till late at night. Days in port are obviously easier as most of the passengers will be ashore.

I suppose most crew members see the world in their twenties and then settle down to have a family. As a divorced parent of a grown-up son, I'm doing it the other way around. The fact that most of my colleagues tend to be younger than me, especially the female ones, means suitable companionship can be a problem on occasions. But in general I enjoy the lifestyle. I feel my maturity lends a certain credence to the job, and older passengers prefer a hostess to whom they can easily relate. It is also to my advantage that I am not prepared to accept conditions that I might have put up with 20 years ago, and the company knows this. It gives me stronger bargaining power.

As the only hostess on this ship, I earn $3,000 a month. I have a spacious single cabin with steward service, free drinks allowance and laundry services. Most evenings I eat in the passenger restaurant, I often go free on any excursions that interest me and I have full public rooms privileges. However not everyone gets this sort of deal. I would say, as a general rule, the more hostesses a vessel has, the worse conditions are offered. I know of ships employing up to fifteen hostesses, each allocated separate tasks from office work to childminding and even security. In circumstances like these, the employees are nearly always in their early twenties, are expected to share cabins and are paid between $800 and $1,200 per month.

If I'm honest, I suppose the hardest aspect of my job is finding time for myself. Even ashore, passengers recognise me and engage me in conversation. Being nice to people twenty-four hours a day, seven days a week can wear you down. Even the continuous round of social functions, such as the Captain's private parties, becomes humdrum after a while, although it does give me an excuse to indulge in my passion for clothes. On an average cruise we might have three 'formal' parties, four 'informal' ones and three 'casual' evenings, labelled according to the suggested evening dress code. Nowadays there is a trend towards less formal wear for cruising, but of course much depends on the ship and the itinerary. As the hostess on a recent World Cruise, I got through twenty different evening gowns — and that was travelling light!

Margot Lawton (age 48)

In the Words of a Cruise Director

I first started on ships about ten years ago as an entertainer in an international musical act. When the act disbanded I was offered the position of Social Directress for a major cruise line and since then I've done most jobs in the social and entertainment sector.

My average day frequently includes a series of meetings: with the Captain, the Hotel Manager or other Heads of Department; continuous faxes and telephone calls to and from our shoreside offices; and scheduling each day's entire programme of activities and events, including checking the proofs of the Daily Programme from the printer. I also present lectures on the ports of call and onboard procedures such as disembarkation, together with introducing the nightly shows and other activities and attending every major cocktail party.

Above all, I am in charge of a department of about 25 people, including the musicians, entertainers, children's counsellors, fitness instructor, DJ and cruise staff members. I am also responsible for a floating (pardon the pun) staff of guest lecturers and clergy members, gentlemen hosts and short-stay headlining cabaret acts.

The downside of this hectic schedule is that I'm constantly in demand — my phone rings even in the middle of the night — and being in the midst of the passengers most of the day can be extremely tiring. I also seem to spend a lot of time attempting to resolve the professional and sometimes, personal problems of members of my department. Occasionally I have had to fire people, which is never easy.

Fortunately, there are also many perks attached to my position. I have senior officer status and appropriate benefits such as a top-grade cabin and generous entertaining allowance, a worldwide circle of interesting friends and associates, including international entertainers and celebrity speakers, and an annual income that I would find hard to match on land. I am also frequently entertained by shoreside agents and tour operators, which gives me the perfect opportunity to indulge in my hobby of discovering good restaurants.

My advice to aspiring Cruise Directors would be to learn how the department runs and get an inside perspective by working in as many areas of the Cruise Staff/Entertainment sector as possible. It is such a specialised job that relevant shipboard experience is vital. I would also say that management skills and the ability to handle people effectively are more important than academic qualifications (although many cruise directors, including myself, do have degrees, though often in quite unrelated subjects).

As one of a minority of female cruise directors, I must also agree with the theory that women at sea sometimes have more to prove than their male counterparts in order to achieve the same promotion. Certainly, females don't tend to be taken as seriously when it comes to long-term careers and, in many ways, it's a Catch 22. They don't get promoted and so they quit, and because they keep quitting, they don't get promoted. I see this particularly in areas such as the Purser's Office, where young women come and go, before you've had time to learn their names.

Yes, I suppose the price of working on ships can be higher for women than men, and not all females are prepared to pay that price. Motherhood and a career at sea are definitely incompatible. Because few continue seafaring beyond the age of about 40, a lack of suitable companionship can be a problem for more mature women. Furthermore men may be intimidated by higher-ranking females (even if they don't admit it) which can limit romantic possibilities. But for women seeking both social and financial independence, a career on cruise ships can be very rewarding.

From a personal point of view I, like many of my colleagues, have several onshore business interests which allow me the financial freedom to choose not to stay on ships if I wished. But like many of my colleagues, I always say I'm not coming back to do yet another six-month contract, and after two months on leave, I always do!

Christine Little (age 34)

Showbusiness

While theatres close down and venues on shore feature less live entertainment, the cruise industry provides performers with an increasingly valuable floating platform for their talents. Most ships present a varied programme of daily and nightly entertainment, including music for dancing, production shows and featured musicians and cabaret acts.

Some cruise lines, such as P&O, Royal Caribbean Cruise Line and Crystal Cruises, mount their own elaborate theatrical productions in-house, while others utilise external production companies to provide a programme of non-stop musical shows.

Either way, various opportunities exist for all-round *Actor/Singer/Dancers* as well as occasional work for *Choreographers* and *Musical Directors*. There are also many openings for *Show Dancers* (especially female). It should be noted, however, that it is commonplace for dancers and production show artists to be expected to assist with general cruise staff duties as well as performing on stage.

Featured Entertainers such as headlining cabaret acts and solo musicians on the other hand are generally not expected to assist with cruise staff or any other duties beside their featured shows (although it must be said that this is gradually changing). Musical, magical and visual speciality acts are particularly popular with cruise lines, due to their international appeal and ability to cut across language barriers.

Ballroom Dance Couples are an attraction on many ships, to teach group classes as part of the activity programme and perform occasional featured routines during the course of each cruise. Some general cruise staff duties may also be expected and, at the artists' discretion, freelance dance lessons given for a privately negotiated fee.

Cruising is still one of the few areas of showbusiness to offer regular employment to *Dance Band Musicians*. Most ships will have at least one or two live bands offering different styles of music from Jazz to Ballroom and the latest in Rock & Roll and Pop. Main Lounge/Theatre Showband

84

SAMPLE DAILY PROGRAMME

Sunrise: 5.50am		Sunset: 5.39pm

AT SEA   **Thursday, 11th January, 1996**   **AT SEA**

FITNESS WITH OUR INSTRUCTOR, LIZ

8.00am	Good Morning Stretch Class - Spa	2.00pm	Beginners Aerobics - Spa
8.30am	Walk a Mile - Jogging Track	3.00pm	Below the Belt! (Hips & Thighs) - Spa
9.15am	Step Aerobics - Spa	5.30pm - 7.30pm	B.C.A./Personal Training - Spa

9.00am - 11.00am Eye Openers! Screwdriver, Bloody Mary - $2.50 — Pool Bar, Deck 8
9.00am Jigsaw Mania continues! — Outside the Calypso Bar, Deck 5
9.00am Daily Quiz is available. Post your answers in the box - earliest top score — Library, Deck 7
wins a prize! (Answers posted tomorrow)
9.30am Bridge players meet your lecturer, Bill — Card Room, Deck 8

9.30am **EARLY BIRD TEAM TRIVIA** — Showtime Lounge, Deck 5
with the Cruise Staff

10.00am Napkin Folding Demonstration with the Restaurant Staff — Neptune's Lounge, Deck 5
10.00am Ping Pong Tournament with the Cruise Staff — Sun Deck, Deck 8
10.00am Junior Cruisers' Treasure Hunt with Children's Auntie, Janice — Rainbow Playroom, Deck 8
10.00am Spanish for Beginners with our International Hostess, Renata — Calypso Bar, Deck 5
10.00am Handwriting Analysis with your lecturer, Bertha — Stardust Disco, Deck 8

10.30am **WHAT TO SEE, WHERE TO GO** — Showtime Lounge, Deck 5
with your **Cruise Director, Tom,** and **Tour Manager, Leslie.**
Lecture on the forthcoming ports of call, including useful hints and advice plus a review of the
Shore Excursions on offer.
(This lecture will be broadcast on Channel 16 at 1.00pm and 2.30pm today)

11.00am Service Club Meeting (Lions, Kiwanis, Rotarians, etc.) — Library, Deck 7
11.00am Arts and Crafts with your lecturer, Noreen — Neptune's Lounge, Deck 5

11.15am **THE MATCH GAME!** — Stardust Disco, Deck 8
Join your Cruise Staff for this hilarious game show!

11.15am MILEAGE POOL! Guess the distance travelled since leaving port — Pool Bar, Deck 8
till noon today - $2 per guess. Meet your Cruise Staff
11.30am Shuffleboard Tournament with the Cruise Staff — Sun Deck, Deck 8

11.30am **GRANDPARENTS GET-TOGETHER** — Calypso Bar, Deck 5
with your **Hostess, Sally** - bring your photos!

11.30am How to play Blackjack - with our Casino Staff — Casino, Deck 5
11.30am Make-up Seminar. Handy hints from our onboard Beauticians — Beauty Salon, Deck 8
11.45am - 1.30pm Lunchtime melodies with our pianist, Alistair — Atrium, Deck 4
12 noon Midday navigational information will be broadcast from the bridge

2.00pm	**CATCH THE SCENT**	Showtime Lounge, Deck 5
	A Perfume Seminar	
	presented by our onboard **Duty Free Shops**	

2.00pm	Bridge Tournament with Bill	Card Room, Deck 8
2.00pm	Scrabble Tournament with your Cruise Staff	Calypso Bar, Deck 5

2.15PM	ICE CARVING DEMONSTRATION with our Chefs	Poolside, Deck 8

2.15pm	Arts and Crafts with Noreen	Neptune's Lounge, Deck 5
2.15pm	LINE DANCING with your Hostess, Sally	Stardust Disco, Deck 8
2.30pm	Kids meet Janice!	Rainbow Playroom, Deck 8

2.45pm	**HORSE RACING**	Showtime Lounge, Deck 5
	with your Cruise Director, Tom	
	Have a flutter at our Whacky Races! Big Cash Prizes!	

2.45pm	Materials and ideas for tomorrow's Fancy Dress Competition	
	are available from the Cruise Staff	Atrium, Deck 4
3.00pm	NAME THAT TUNE! Musical Quiz with our DJ, Paul	Stardust Disco, Deck 8
3.00pm	Deck Quoits Tournament with our Cruise Staff	Sun Deck, Deck 8

3.00pm	**POOL-ING AROUND!**	Poolside, Deck 8
	Fun and Games with our Production Show Team!	

3.15pm	Oriental Cookery Demonstration with our Chefs	Neptune's Lounge, Deck 5
3.30pm	American Roulette lessons with our Croupiers	Casino, Deck 5
3.30pm	Wine & Cheese tasting (nominal charge of $5.00 per person)	Calypso Bar, deck 5

3.30pm	**JACKPOT BINGO**	Showtime Lounge, Deck 5
	More Cash Prizes to be Won!	

4.00pm	AFTERNOON TEA is served until 5.00pm	Palm Court Café, Deck 7
4.30pm	Chess Tournament with the Cruise Staff	Card Room, Deck 8

4.30pm	**LIAR'S CLUB!**	Showtime Lounge, Deck 5
	Join your **Cruise Director** and **his Staff** for this fun-filled **Game Show!**	

5.00pm	HAPPY HOUR! Two drinks for the price of one! (until 6.30pm)	Calypso Bar, Deck 5
5.00pm	Early evening melodies with Alistair at the piano	Calypso Bar, Deck 5

5.30pm	**SINGLES MINGLE**	Neptune's Lounge, Deck 5
	Travelling Solo? Join your Hostess, Sally, and fellow guests	

5.30pm	**Dance to the Big Band Sounds**	Showtime Lounge, Deck 5
	of the **Mike Davidson Orchestra**	

7.15pm - 8.30pm	**MUSIC FOR DANCING**	Neptune's Lounge, Deck 5
9.30pm - 10.30pm	with the **Dave Peters Trio**	

86

| 7.45pm | **FASHION SHOW** | Showtime Lounge, Deck 5 |

Our Gift Shop Manager and Staff model Clothing
and Accessories from our onboard Duty Free Shops

8.45pm - 1st Sitting   Showtime Lounge, Deck 5
10.30pm - 2nd Sitting

SHOWTIME

starring

The Comedy-Magic of
DANNY & DENISE

and

The Multi-Musical Talents of
PIETRO BARROLI

Accompanied by The Mike Davidson Orchestra

Thank you for not smoking during the performances. Videotaping is not permitted

| 10.00pm | **DANCE UNTIL THE EARLY HOURS**
with our DJ, Paul | Stardust Disco, Deck 8 |

| 9.30pm - 1.00am | **MUSIC FOR DANCING**
with
MOOD INDIGO | Neptune's Lounge, Deck 5 |

| 7.45pm - 8.45pm
9.45pm - 11.00pm | **EVENING COCKTAIL MELODIES**
with our pianist, Alistair | Calypso Bar, Deck 5 |

11.45pm - 12.30am   LATE NIGHT BUFFET is served!   Trident Restaurant

TODAY'S MOVIES

CHANNEL 16	Broadcast of this morning's Port and Travel Talk at 11.00pm and 2.30pm
CHANNEL 16	**BRAVEHEART** (Historical adventure starring Mel Gibson - PG13) 7.30am, 10.00am, 4.00pm, 6.30pm, 9.00pm and 11.30pm)
CHANNEL 28	**CASPER** (Comedy starring Christina Ricci - PG) 7.30am, 9.30am, 11.30am, 2.00pm, 4.00pm, 6.00pm, 8.00pm, 10.00pm and 12 midnight

ONBOARD DINING

Breakfast	7.00am - 7.30am	Early risers coffee and pastries in the Palm Court Café
	7.00am - 9.00am	Open Sitting Breakfast in the Trident Restaurant
	7.30am - 10.00am	Breakfast Buffet in the Palm Court Café
Snack	10.30am - 11.15am	Hot Bouillon and Crackers in the Palm Court Café
Lunch	12 noon	1st Sitting Lunch in the Trident Restaurant
	1.30pm	2nd Sitting Lunch in the Trident Restaurant
	12.30pm - 2.30pm	Buffet Lunch in the Palm Court Café
	4.00pm - 4.45pm	Afternoon Tea in the Palm Court Café
Dinner	6.00pm	1st Sitting Dinner in the Trident Restaurant
	8.30pm	2nd Sitting Dinner in the Trident Restaurant
Buffet	11.45pm - 12.45pm	Late Night Buffet in the Trident Restaurant

BAR HOURS

Calypso Bar	9.00am - Close
Pool Bar	9.00am - 6.00pm
Neptune's Lounge	5.00pm - Close
Showtime Lounge	7.30pm - Close
Stardust Disco	10.00pm - Close

DEPARTMENT HOURS AND TELEPHONE NUMBERS

Purser's Office, Deck 5 - Tel: 0	Open 24 Hours
Shore Excursion Office, Deck 5 - Tel: 5423	11.00am - 2.00pm and 7.00pm - 8.30pm
Hospital Surgery Hours, Deck 2 - Tel: 5000	9.00am - 11.00am and 5.30pm - 6.30pm
Gift Shops, Deck 5 - Tel: 5682	9.00am - 12 noon, 2.00pm - 6.00pm and 8.00pm - 10.00pm
Duty Free Liquor Shop, Deck 8 - Tel: 5121	9.00am - 12 noon, 2.00pm - 6.00pm and 8.00pm - 10.00pm
Beauty Salon, Deck 8 - Tel: 5480	8.00am - 8.00pm
Spa and Gymnasium, Deck 8 - Tel: 5771	8.00am - 8.00pm
Photo Gallery, Deck 4 - Tel: 5232	11.00am - 12 noon and 4.00pm - 5.00pm
Casino, Deck 5 - Tel: 5569	9.00am (Slots) and 2.00pm (Tables) - Close

Photo Gallery: To order photos, fill out an order form (available at the Photo Gallery) with your name, cabin number and the code number of the displayed photo(s) of your choice. Drop the form in the Photo Order Box and your photos will be delivered to your cabin by the end of the cruise. 35mm film can also be processed on board. Ask our photographer for details.

Gift Shops: Take a look at our loose gemstones -amethyst, Citrine and Blue Topaz. Only $10 per carat and all with certificates from the Gemological Board of Trade.

members should also be good sight readers as they may frequently be requested to back headlining acts and production shows.

Lounge Bar Musicians and *Cocktail Pianists* are particularly in demand, as even the smallest ships may require a talented pianist or duo for their intimate lounge or piano bar. Subject to a ship's itinerary, speciality musical groups such as calypso bands may also be required.

Self-contained *Featured Musicians* (such as harpists, accordionists, xylophonists and even zither players) are occasionally required on larger vessels. *Opera Singers, Concert Pianists* and other *Classical Musicians* (e.g. string quartets) may be employed to give recitals and concert performances, especially during themed Classical Music and World cruises. Openings here are fairly limited, however, and trained singers may find more regular work as part of a shipboard production show.

Many opportunities exist for professional Disc Jockeys. Note, however, that salaries and conditions vary enormously from company to company and ship to ship, and often the DJ will be expected to assist with other aspects of the entertainment programme, including cruise staff duties.

Addresses of Entertainment Agencies

For work as a musician, ballroom dance couple, DJ or headlining act, contact the entertainment department of the respective cruise lines or the many theatrical and musical agencies which specialise in booking ships. This is just a selection of the many agents and producers active in the cruise ship market. It is also worth consulting theatrical newspapers, particularly *The Stage* and *Television Today* in the UK.

Salaries, as in all areas of show business, will be individually negotiated and can range from $300 (£200) per week for a youthful dancer to $2,000 (£1,350) and up for an established featured act. Agents move in and out of favour, so it is worth checking with the cruise lines which ones they are currently using before applying. Agents, specialising in the cruise market, include:

Allan Blackburn, Le Montaigne, 2 Avenue de la Madone, 98000 Monte Carlo, France. Tel: 93 30 67 98.

Bramson Productions, 1501 Broadway, New York, NY 10036, USA. Tel: 212-354-9575 (Entertainment) or 212-391-4646 (Productions).

Elaine Avon Ltd, 'Montage', 127 Westhall Rd, Warlingham, Surrey CR3 9HJ. Tel: 01883 622317.

Fiesta Fantastica, 230 SW 8th St, Miami, FL 33130, USA. Tel: 305-854-2221.

Garry Brown Associates, 27 Downs Side, Cheam, Surrey SM2 7EH. Tel: 0181-673 3991/8375.

Matrix Entertainments Ltd, PO Box 70, Oxshott, Surrey KT22 OHS. Tel: 01372 464829.

Meyer Davis Agency, West 57th St, New York, NY 10019, USA. Tel: 212-247-6161. For musicians only.

Roger Kendrick Entertainment, National Westminster Bank Chambers,

6 Orchard Road, St. Annes-on-Sea, Lancs, FY8 1RH. Tel: 01253 726046.

Ship Services International Inc (see address above under *Addresses of Cruise Staff Employers*).

Showcase Entertainments, 63 North Hill, Colchester, Essex. Tel: 01206 571311.

Showmasters, 3038-D North Federal Highway, Fort Lauderdale, FL 33306, USA. Tel: 305-563-8028.

Tube Productions, 5253 Decarie Boulevard, Montreal, Quebec H3W 3CZ, Canada. Tel: 514-485-8823. Musicians mainly.

For work as a singer, actor or dancer, try the following production companies. British performers should note that many American-based companies also hold regular auditions in Great Britain.

Jean Anne Ryan Productions, 308 SE 14th St, Fort Lauderdale, FL 33316, USA. Tel: 305-523-6399.

Marcello Productions, Fiesta Fantastica Inc, 230 SW 8th St, Miami, FL 33130, USA. Tel: 305-854-2221.

Peter Grey Terhune Productions, PO Box 715, Cape Canaveral, FL 32920, USA. Tel: 407-783-8745.

Ray Kennedy Production Company, 244 South Academy St, Mooresville, North Carolina 28115, USA. Tel: 704-662-3501.

Stadium Theatre Company, c/o P & O Cruises, Richmond House, Terminus Terrace, Southampton SO14 3PN, Hampshire. Tel: 01703 534200.

In the Words of a Dancer

I'm a dancer in a shipboard production show, along with seven other performers, four female and three male. Four of us are from different parts of the United States, one is Canadian and two are from Great Britain, so we're quite an international cast. Although our company is based in Florida, dancers from Europe and Britain in particular have such a good reputation that a lot of American producers audition in cities such as London, Manchester and Paris, as well as in the US. My two colleagues from England attended an audition in London. We all met up for the first time in Fort Lauderdale where we spent three weeks rehearsing before joining the ship. Of course, our company paid for our flights and provided our food and accommodation, together with a rehearsal salary, during this time.

There's a lot of competition for work as a dancer on ships and most companies like you to be able to sing as well. All seven of us are good all-rounders, but the two principals are trained singers who can move, rather than great dancers. All the vocals are performed live and the band accompanies us by following a 'click-track', so the tempos are the same for every show.

On each cruise we do three different shows with two perform-ances of each show (for first and second dinner sittings). This week we've also been rehearsing a lot for a new fourth show. It can sometimes be difficult to schedule practice times because the show lounge is also used for other activities, so we may have to rehearse at lunchtimes or even midnight. This can be hard if we then have to get up early the next day to help with cruise staff duties, even if the tasks are fairly easy like decorating for theme nights or assisting with games and activities.

My contract is for six months but I will probably accept an offer to extend it, mainly to be with my boyfriend, Carlos. He is from Panama and works as the head bartender in the main lounge where we do our shows. I like him because he's different from most of the other straight guys on this ship. In fact, he's the only bartender who didn't make a pass at me in my first week. As a girl dancer, you get a lot of attention from the men onboard which can be flattering at first. But you soon realise that most of them only see you as 'fresh meat' and as soon as other girls come on the scene, they quickly lose interest. The three guys in our show are all gay so they're not interested in us anyway.

Some entertainers may think that working at sea is inferior to performing on land, but I disagree. Many ships now have full-scale theatres onboard, complete with all kinds of special lighting and sound effects, and shipboard production shows are becoming more and more sophisticated, often rivalling shows on Broadway or in London's West End. Besides, so many of my colleagues on land are struggling for work that I feel lucky to be here. Who wants to starve in Manhattan when you can be paid to perform and travel the world at the same time?

Mandy-Jo Murphy (age 19)

What's Your Line: Opportunities for Experts

Do you have any special skills, hobbies or unusual claims to fame? And would you be able to pass on your knowledge or expertise to other people? If the answer is yes, you might like to consider applying to be a *Guest Lecturer* at sea. Don't be put off by the academic-sounding title. You don't need teaching qualifications to do this, simply the ability to do something well and the confidence to tell or show an audience of passengers how you do it.

There is a hitch, however: you don't get paid. What you do get is a free or substantially-reduced cruise for yourself and a companion with full passenger status and accommodation in return for just a few hours of work. Neither is there an upper age limit. Many guest lecturers are retired and some 'work their passage' several times a year.

Scope for Fortune-Telling

The most common specialist subjects are Contract Bridge, Arts and Crafts, Self-improvement (Positive Thinking, Health & Beauty, How to Combat Stress, Improve Your Memory, etc.), Fortune-Telling (including Palmistry and Tarot cards), Handwriting Analysis, Portrait and Caricature Drawing, and Golf Instruction. Leading exponents in a particular field may also give Celebrity Lectures. Airline pilots, media personalities, mountaineers, archaeologists, antiques and gardening experts have all found an audience among cruise passengers.

Check through holiday brochures for ships that offer theme cruises that may be relevant to your area of work or interest. Look in particular at the programmes of specialist and 'explorer' cruises with companies such as Abercrombie & Kent or Classical Cruises (see *Cruise Line Addresses*) at end of book).

If you contact the cruise lines direct, do enquire about their policies regarding guest lecturers (as their requirements are subject to change) before bombarding them with samples of your work. Bear in mind too the feasibility of your chosen topic, considering you will be expected to provide and transport any materials or photographic slides that you intend using (and this includes materials for instructing purposes if you intend to give classes in an art or craft).

Often, cruise companies use employment agencies that specialise in supplying guest lecturers to ships. The head office of the respective lines should be able to tell you which agents (if any) they use for your specific line of expertise. But don't forget, if you obtain work through an agency they will charge you a placement fee which, on top of other expenses such as the cost of flights to join the ship, may make your working holiday more expensive than you had envisaged.

One of the larger agencies handling general guest lecturers is: Program Experts, Inc, 50 Spring St, Suite 6, PO Box 510, Cresskill, New Jersey 07626-0510 (tel 201-569-7950). You could also try Karp Enterprises, 2139 University Drive, Coral Springs, FL 33071 (tel 305-341-9400).

Jobs for the Boys: Gentlemen Hosts

Cruise lines are in need of older gentleman who are smart, articulate, well-travelled, well-read, good conversationalists and, above all, good ballroom dancers. This is because the number of female passengers on the average cruise invariably outweighs the number of males and a highlight for many of the ladies is the chance to dance the night away. Gentlemen Hosts are therefore in great demand as companions and especially as dancing partners, in return for a free or subsidised cruise on much the same terms as the Guest Lecturers.

Don't be fooled into thinking that an occasional glide round the dance floor will suffice. The emphasis will be more on work than on holiday. But if you have poise, charm and a strong pair of dancing shoes, the larger ships at the more upmarket end of the industry may be particularly interested in hearing from you. Try especially Cunard Line, Crystal Cruises, Ivaran Lines, Holland America Line and Royal Cruise Line (RCL). Also try the specialist Lauretta Blake Agency, 4277 Lake Santa Clara Drive, Santa Clara, CA 95054-1330 (tel 408-727-9665).

Shore Excursions: Work in the Tour Sector

On some ships, the sale and marketing of organised shore excursions may fall under the umbrella of the cruise staff department, while on others the Shore Excursions (Tour) Office is a separate department under the direction of an experienced *Shore Excursions Manager* (or similar-sounding title). By liaising with the ship's agents in each port of call, the Shore Excursions Manager will ensure the smooth running of the whole programme of optional or included tours, from the reservation of coaches and local guides to the sale of tickets. Although Tour Office personnel frequently escort excursions, there are no real opportunities for Tour Guides at sea as local guides are generally used in the various ports of call.

Shore excursion work is an interesting job, socially as well as professionally. An added perk is that local agents and tour company personnel are very eager to entertain and reward you for bringing business their way.

Opportunities also exist for *Shore Excursions (Tour) Office Assistants,*

Gentleman host are in demand

especially on larger ships where a whole team of staff may be employed in this capacity. Experience is not necessarily a requirement here, although previous work in the travel industry would be helpful.

Monthly salaries range from $1,500 (£1,000) for assistants to $3,000 (£2,000) and upwards for managers, and there may be commission-making opportunities. For newcomers to ships who are interested in the tourism and excursion angle, a job as a Tour Office Assistant can be an excellent starting point.

For work in this sector, apply directly to each cruise company. One exception is the Holland America Line which has its own affiliated company (Westours) at the same address which recruits tour staff: 300 Elliott Avenue West, Seattle, Washington 98119 (tel 206-281-3535).

Concessionaires

Many cruise lines make use of specialist companies and agencies to supply some of the services and staff needed on a ship. Many, if not most, of the employees in the Hotel Department of a ship work for a company other than the cruise line itself. In other words, they work for a company which has an onboard concession, known as 'concessionaires'. Catering has already provided us with a good example of this (see section *Catering Concessionaires*). But, outside the restaurant, many areas of the ship are staffed by employees of concessionaires, principally the retail shops, beauty salons, fitness centres and casinos.

Catering apart, all the people who work in the various concessions fall into the classification of staff, as distinct from officers and crew. They are paid directly by the company which hired them, although they are bound by the rules and conditions of the ship. Unlike people employed directly by the ship they often make a contribution for their living expenses. But in most cases they get much more free time in port than people working in other capacities. Staff who work under customs regulations, for example in the on-board duty-free shop, boutiques and casino, are free to go ashore when the ship is not sailing.

RETAIL SHOPS

Why be a *Shop Assistant* in town, when you can be a shop assistant all over the world? If you have retail experience, especially in the duty free or department store sector, there could be openings here for you. All reasonably-sized ships have at least one retail outlet onboard and large ships may have a whole shopping arcade, selling a vast range of duty free goods, clothes, cosmetics, necessities and gifts.

Often these shops are run by famous High Street companies. Allders have a strong shipping division with concessions on various leading lines. Harrods have branches on only two ships to date, the *QE2* (Cunard Line) and the *Oriana* (P & O Cruises) and tends to recruit from their own onshore employees. Obviously anyone who is already employed by such a company has an advantage. But others can consider approaching the relevant personnel officer and asking about vacancies in the store's branches at sea.

Good *Sales Assistants*, including experienced *Shop Managers*, are in demand on ships, especially those who speak more than one language. Salaries are generally comparable with shoreside retail earnings and include incentives. The most promising companies to approach directly for this kind of work are P & O Cruises, Princess Cruises, Carnival Cruise Lines and Louis Cruise Lines (a Cyprus-based company with several ships and a duty free shopping chain). See *Cruise Line Addresses* at end of book.

Don't forget to consider the ferry companies, such as Stena Sealink, P & O European Ferries and Brittany Ferries etc. also listed at the end of this book.

Window Dressing

There are virtually no opportunities for *Window Dressers* to work on a ship for more than a couple of days (or even hours) at a time. But concessionaires may employ staff specifically to travel between ships, changing and updating displays during the few hours that a liner is in port. This affords exciting travel opportunities for experienced Window Dressers who are able to be creative under pressure and still meet seemingly impossible deadlines. If this is your area of expertise, contact the concessionary companies below.

Addresses of Shop Concessionaires

The following companies place retail staff on various lines. Specialist agencies to try include:

Allders International (Ships) Ltd, 84/98 Southampton Road, Eastleigh, Hants. SO5 5ZF. Tel: 01703 644599. Also in US: 1510 17th St, Fort

Lauderdale, FL 33316 (tel: 305-763-8551). The foremost company in this field.

Apollo Ship Chandlers (address in section *Catering Concessionaires).*

Clerici Cruise Services, PO Box 121, 2335 NW 107th Avenue, Miami, FL 33172, USA. Tel: 305-763-8551.

Harrod's (Cruising), Personnel Dept, 87-135 Brompton Road, London SW1X 7XL. Tel: 0171-730 1234.

International Cruise Shops, 8052 NW 14th St, Miami, FL 33126, USA. Tel: 305-592-6460. Division of Greyhound Leisure, which also provides Bar Staff.

Suncoast Cruise Services, 2335 NW 107th Avenue, Miami, FL 33172. Tel: 305-591-1763.

VIP International (address in section *Catering Concessionaires)*

In the Words of a Gift Shop Assistant

For the past year and a half I've been employed as a gift shop assistant onboard a Caribbean-based cruise ship. Like most retail staff on ships I work for an independent concessionaire rather than for the cruise line itself and, because of this, I personally have to contribute about $60 (£42) per week towards the cost of my board, which I pay direct to the Crew Purser on the ship.

When I originally applied for this position I was already working on the cosmetics counter of a large department store in my home town of Manchester. I'm sure it was mainly because of this practical experience that I was offered the job, since at that time I'd never even set foot on a ship and didn't really know what to expect.

I must admit, when I first saw my cabin I couldn't believe how small it was. I now realise that I'd packed far too many clothes, especially as my company provides me with a uniform for work and I only wear casual summer clothes ashore. I have to share the cabin with one of the other 'shoppies' and fortunately we get on really well, in spite of the fact we'd never met before. It helps that her boyfriend is an engineer with his own cabin, so I often have the place to myself.

We are allocated a steward, who cleans and makes our beds each day, but we have to take our uniforms to the laundry ourselves. Our uniforms are cleaned free of charge and there are also free washers and dryers in the crew areas but the machines are in such demand that it's often quicker to rinse things out by hand and hang them in our shower to dry.

Although my cabin is in a crew area, I do have 'public rooms privileges' (as all gift shop assistants do), which means I can use passenger facilities such as the pool and the gymnasium (at off-peak times) and the passenger lounges and bars. I often join other staff members and officers in the passenger disco after work, as it's a nicer option than the crew bar and we get a good discount on drinks.

I suppose my bar bills and taxi fares to the beach are my only real expenses at the moment, which is why, for the first time in my life, I'm able to save money. I earn a basic of $200 (approximately £135) per week plus commission if we make our sales target. On 'target' weeks I'll treat myself to something special onshore. On that subject, I do get quite a lot of time off in exotic places.

Of course it's not all palm trees and cocktails. On days at sea the shops are open from early in the morning till late at night. I dread certain tasks like stocktaking and the arrival of new supplies on embarkation days. I also hate the weekly crew safety drill as I'm sometimes asked to help lower a lifeboat. But in the main, I enjoy my job and prefer it to working on land. Yes, there are times when I get homesick but after a few days on leave I get sick of home!

Andrea Gordon (age 24)

HAIR & BEAUTY SALONS

Most cruise ships will have their own onboard Hair and Beauty Salon and some may even boast a sophisticated Health and Beauty Centre, equipped with the very latest technology. *Salon Managers, Hairdressers, Beauticians, Manicurists, Masseurs* and *Masseuses* are therefore in great demand and larger vessels may also have openings for *Chiropodists* and *Physiotherapists* (see also the next section *Spas & Fitness Centres* and also *Medical Department*).

If you wish to apply for any type of work in this sector you should be qualified and experienced before climbing the gangway, as there are generally no openings for trainees in shipboard salons. As with all applications, the more versatile you appear to be, the greater your chance of acceptance. Beauticians who can manicure, masseuses who can make-up, hairdressers who can style both the normal and the very formal, these are the types of people employers are seeking.

It has to be said that salon salaries are not the highest on the seven seas, with earnings starting at around $600 (£400) per month. But there is potential for making reasonable tips. Not to mention the appeal of doing a blow-dry in Bali rather than a blue rinse in Balham.

The major salon concessionaires are Steiners, Allders International, Golden Door and Champneys; see the next section *Spas and Fitness*

Centres for the addressess. Note that Steiners (now incorporating Coiffeur Transocean) sometimes offer lower salaries than some others but, with its London-based training school and high staff requirements, also offers more opportunities for newcomers.

SPAS AND FITNESS CENTRES

Spas are becoming an increasingly popular feature of luxury cruise ships, with many modern liners possessing highly sophisticated hydrotherapy, fitness and sauna facilities. Sometimes the spa operates in conjunction with the beauty salon and is run by the same parent company. In other cases it is operated by a separate concessionaire. Some ships' gymnasiums are affiliated to the spa, while others are controlled by the cruise line itself. Needless to say, this can become rather confusing and it is worth checking to whom you should apply before sending off your details.

As a generalisation, positions exist for experienced *Spa Managers*, qualified *Masseurs/Masseuses, Spa Assistants* with a good working knowledge of the latest hydrotherapy, relaxation and detoxification techniques, qualified *Gymnasium Supervisors, Fitness and/or Aerobics Instructors* who can offer personal health and fitness programmes (see also *Entertainment* chapter), and qualified and experienced *Physiotherapists*. Salaries are generally comparable to those in land-based health and fitness facilities, and in some cases even lower.

Addresses of Beauty & Fitness Concessionaires

Allders International (Ships) Ltd, (see address above under *Retail Shops*).
Champneys Health Club, Le Meridien, Piccadilly, London W1V OBH. Tel: 0171-437 8114.
Golden Door, PO Box 463077, Escondido, California 92046-3077, USA. Tel: 619-744-5777.
Steiner Beauty Therapy School/Maritime Academy, 66 Grosvenor St, London W1X OAX. Tel: 0171-493 1146 or 0171-495 7115. Also, Steiner Group Ltd, Personnel Dept, 57-65 The Broadway, Stanmore, Middlesex HA7 4DU. Tel: 0181-954 6121.
The Stylists, 4644 Kolohala St, Honolulu, Hawaii 96815, USA. Tel: 808-923-4477. Employs mainly US citizens.

In the Words of a Fitness Instructor

> *During the two years that I have worked as a fitness instructor at sea, I have worked on three different ships and have cruised Alaska, South America, the Bahamas, and now the Caribbean. And yes, I really enjoy the life. Before I came to sea I was working*

in a private health club near my home in Essex, and also acting as a coach at a local sports centre. This experience, together with about fifteen related Health and Fitness qualifications, definitely helped me to get the job. Qualifications are important and any British instructors wishing to teach fitness at sea should at least have passed the RSA (Royal Society of Arts) Exercise to Music, be qualified in NABA (National Association of Bodybuilders and Athletes) personal training programmes, including BCA (Body Composition Analysis), and be fully trained in CPR and First Aid.

On the ship, I'm responsible for my own programme of classes, which I try to make as balanced as possible. I also have to gear my classes to the variable standard of the students, remembering that cruise ship passengers are generally older and less active than the fitness students I teach onshore. The morning 'walk-a-mile' around the deck is really popular and a surprising number of passengers come to the daily stretch class. I also get a mixture of active younger passengers, especially those who work out regularly at home, who want me to devise personal training programmes for them. Although use of the spa and gymnasium is free, I charge for consultations, and this can make a big difference to my $220 (£150) weekly 'basic'. The money is actually worse than I could make on land, but it's a great way to see the world. The concessionaire I work for pays for my flights and expenses, and I manage to save far more than I ever did at home. But I would advise would-be instructors who are offered a choice between working direct for a cruise line as a member of cruise staff or working for a spa concessionaire to go for the cruise staff option as the money and conditions are usually better and you're not bound by the rules and hours of the spa and beauty salon.

I suppose the thing I find the hardest about my job at sea is keeping up with the fitness industry itself. It's easy to get isolated in your own little floating gym and get out of touch with the latest equipment and techniques. For this reason, I get my family to send me copies of trade magazines and, when I go back on leave, I always enrol for a few classes and refresher courses. I believe that passing on knowledge and acquiring it go hand in hand. A good instructor never stops learning.

Lesley Davey-Jones (age 25)

CASINOS

If you are over 21 years old and a trained dealer with previous experience you could be onto a winner at sea. Ships' casinos have a high requirement for all kinds of staff: *Managers, Assistant Managers, Pit Bosses, Inspectors, Croupiers, Cashiers* and *Casino Technicians.*

All casinos at sea will have a Manager and possibly even an Assistant Manager, while only the ones with large casinos need Pit Bosses and Inspectors who may in time have the opportunity of being promoted to managerial positions on smaller ships.

Technicians (who must be able to maintain and repair slot machines, etc.) and Cashiers are expected to have appropriate experience, although not necessarily casino experience.

Croupiers must be able to handle both Blackjack and Roulette, while experience of other games like Punto Banco, Poker or Craps is a bonus. A minimum of two years dealing experience is preferred, although exceptions may be made if, for example, the applicant has passed a college course in gaming.

As with all casinos, working hours are anti-social. But there are compensations, including the fact that, due to international gaming laws, casinos on ships are always closed (and therefore the staff are off) in every port of call.

Salaries are frequently lower than those paid by onshore casinos (particularly British ones), but incentives are often offered and tips — often in the form of chips — are not only accepted but expected. Dealers should therefore earn at least $1,000 (£650) per month and managers can generally expect in excess of $3,000 (£2,000).

Useful Contacts for Casino Work

Those who have already acquired some land-based experience should apply to the relevant concessionaires listed below, or check trade magazines, such as *Gaming For British Croupiers*. Those who are looking for the right training should note the following list of croupier training schools whose graduates are often recruited by gaming concessionaires:

Austin Stephens, Roman House, 9/10 College Terrace, Mile End, London E3 5AN. Tel: 0181-980 4279.

International Casino Monitoring, 13a High St, Crayford, Dartford, Kent DA1 4HH. Tel: 01322 554124.

Casino Resource Centre, 2 The Linen House, 253 Kilburn Lane, London W10. Tel: 0181-960 5733.

The following companies all employ staff for casinos at sea. So play your cards right and drop them a line.

The Berkeley Bureau, 11 Cranmer Road, Hampton Hill, Middlesex TW12 1DW. Tel 0181-941 7110.

Casinos Austria Maritime, 200 South Biscayne Boulevard, Suite 1690, Miami, FL 33131, USA. Tel: 305-377-2117.

Gamex, Sedar Cottage, Sedar Road, Woking, Surrey. Tel: 01483 751711.

Greater Atlantic Casinos Ltd, 990 Northwest 166th St, Miami, FL 33169, USA. Tel: 305-359-0001.

London Clubs Ltd, Golden Nugget, 22-32 Shaftesbury Avenue, London W1. Tel: 0181-863 8801.

Mayfair Maritime Casinos, 30 Old Burlington St, London W1. Tel: 0171-637 5464.

Princess Casinos (for Princess Cruises), 10100 Santa Monica Blvd, Los Angeles, California 90067, USA. Tel: 213-553-1770.

Shore Side Consultants, 1007 North America Way, Suite 305, Miami, FL 33132, USA. Tel: 305-381-9544.

Note that Caesar's World Casinos of Caesar's Palace fame in Las Vegas is the concessionaire for Crystal Cruises but they only employ people from their own onshore workforce.

In the Words of a Croupier

I work as a dealer on a cruise ship based in the Bahamas. Our ship specialises in three and four-day party cruises and the passengers are really out to have a good time. They play hard, both in the casino and in the bars, so it tends to be one long party for us too.

We work late, usually until at least 2am, although this depends on how busy we are. Most of the dealers then go to the disco until it closes at 4am. Fortunately, we don't open the tables until the afternoon, so we also get a lie-in. But I would warn newcomers to casinos, and especially casinos at sea, of the danger of getting into a nocturnal lifestyle, whereby you eat breakfast at lunchtime, never see daylight and never get off the ship because you're sleeping through the day. It's easy to lose track of time and, to wake up not knowing whether it's night or day (since most crew cabins don't have portholes). Quite recently, one of our dealers woke at 6 o'clock and, thinking he had overslept for the evening shift, threw on his tuxedo and ran to the casino, only to find it was 6am and his only customer was the night cleaner.

I personally tend to take advantage of the fact that casino staff don't have to work in port, by getting off the ship as much as possible. I'm a keen scuba diver so this itinerary in the Caribbean is perfect for me. I dive whenever I have the chance since I am currently working towards my Master Diver Certificate. When I'm not in the water, I go to the onshore casinos, particularly in Nassau, where I'm friendly with some of the local dealers. It may seem strange to want to spend my free time at the tables, but we're not allowed to gamble in our own casino, and it can be quite refreshing to be a punter for a change.

My advice to would-be dealers is, first of all, get trained. Either approach your local casino and ask if they are recruiting or enrol at a reputable croupier training school. Once you have two games such as roulette and blackjack under your belt and some experience, you are in a position to apply to the cruise lines and casino concessionaires. Since working on ships I have also made a point of learning how to deal dice and stud poker, as the more games you can deal, the better your chances of being accepted by other companies, if and when you need a change.

As a dealer, the world's your oyster and not just on the ships. I have friends who trained at the same casino as I did in London who are now working in Sun City (South Africa), the Bahamas, Australia and the Far East. But for me, cruise ships offer the most exciting lifestyle, and without the expenses of working on land. When I go back home and see my family and friends, everyone seems so hard up. It's as if whatever they earn gets swallowed up by the cost of living. But at sea you're in a continual holiday atmosphere and it's easy to forget about the hard realities. If you're looking for travel, glamour, romance and the chance to save a bit of money, working as a croupier on ships is definitely the answer. It's a great life.

Allan Hicks (age 30)

I see, so its 6 am not 6pm!

SAY CHEESE: Opportunities for Photographers

Professional *Photographers* will find plenty of opportunities on cruise ships, which may have anything from a small single-handed operation to a six or seven-person team under the direction of an experienced Chief Photographer. Applicants should possess a high standard of photographic skills, combined with practical ability and experience in printing and developing. Dark room work, together with the selling of photographs, is often an integral part of the job.

One factor that you should take into account before applying to be a ship's photographer is that you are likely to be working against much tighter deadlines than on land. Thousands of split-second shots of passengers — shaking the Captain's hand, posing for portraits, on the gangway, in the restaurant, from port to port and party to party — all have to be snapped and processed against the clock. And if the photos aren't on the display board by the end of the cruise, you've lost the sale and therefore the commission that forms the bulk of your income. A photographer's 'basic' can be as low as $100 (£65) per week but, with commission, earning potential may well exceed eight times as much. This is also one of the 'fun' jobs on the ship, in the midst of the social scene and with plenty of free time in port.

Maritime Photographic Employers

Anyone interested in this work should keep an eye on trade publications (such as *The Photographer* and the *British Journal of Photography*) for cruise job advertisements or get in touch with the following companies. Who knows? Your next shoot could be on location.

Cruise Ship Picture Company, 1177 South America Way, Suite 200, Miami, FL33132, USA. Tel: 305-539-1903. Contact address in UK: 132 High St, Esher, Surrey KT10 9QB.

JALcruise (UK) Ltd, Unit 7, Home Farm Rural Industries, East Tytherley Road, Lockerley, Romsey, Hants. Tel: 01794 341409. Incorporates Ocean Images (tel: 01794 341818).

Neptune Photographic, 202 Fulham Road, London SW10 9NB. Tel: 0171-351 7181.

Ocean Pictures, Canefield Farmhouse, Lockerley, Romsey, Hants. SO51 OJH. Tel: 01794 342424. Major concessionaire (not connected to JALcruise or Ocean Images of Lockerley).

Trans Ocean Photos, Inc, Suite A, Berth One, NY Passenger Ship Terminal, 711 12th Avenue, New York, NY 10019, USA. Tel: 212-757-2707. Incorporates Trans Ocean Video, Inc).

Try also two cruise lines which hire their photographers direct: Paquet French Cruises (only if you speak reasonble French) and Carnival Cruise Lines (addresses in *Cruise Lines & Operators*.)

In the Words of a Ship's Photographer

I've worked as a Chief Photographer on ships for so long (about seven years) that I've almost forgotten what it was like to do photography on land, even though I started off with a local studio in England doing the usual rounds of weddings, barmitzvahs and 'Bonny Baby' portraits.

On the ship I'm on now, I'm in charge of two other photographers. One is a 20 year old newcomer to cruising and the other has worked with me on two previous ships. The main advantage of being the 'number one' is that I get a better sales percentage than they do. Also I have a cabin to myself, whereas they have to double up. The disadvantage is that I'm responsible for everything to do with the photographic department, including my guys being late for the early morning shots because they are still hung over from the night before.

To be a good ship's photographer is not just a matter of taking a good picture. Although related qualifications, such as a college degree in photography, are certainly advantageous, we are not looking for artistic individualists. Rather, we need flexible all-rounders, people who can work as a team. I stress this because we are living and working together in such confined conditions for such long periods that team spirit and the ability to get along with people is essential. If someone is really technical it's a help, and every team member should be able to develop films, using a Fuji (or similar) lab processor. Our photographers need also to be adept at handling professional-quality cameras by makers such as Nikon, Leica and Hasselblad. I always use my own personal Nikon FM2, and although our company supplies us with additional cameras, I find most of my colleagues also prefer to use their own models.

We operate a rota system of selling the prints, so retail experience is always handy, and we each earn a percentage of the overall sales. This varies between 3% and 7% according to status and length of service with the company. I personally have made over $1,500 (£1,000) per week on some ships, especially on seven to ten-day cruises with interesting itineraries. But every group of passengers is different and on a bad week I may only end up with $400 (£250). You also have to take into account the fact that most photographic concessionaires do not pay your travel expenses to and from the ship, so you are personally responsible for your own flights and this can knock your earnings back. For this reason I always do contracts of at least six months and sometimes nine.

If I'm honest, I think some of the cruise lines are getting greedier at the expense of the concessionaires and, indirectly, the photographers themselves. There is a trend for the lines to operate their own in-house photographic departments, which usually means they cut out the middle-man but pay the staff the same as (or less than) before. Even cruise lines that still use independent companies may expect to take 60%-70% of the revenue, which means the concessionaires then reduce our percentages too.

But in spite of this, cruising can still be both financially and socially rewarding for photographers who want to travel the world in a party atmosphere. Most ships' photogs are in their twenties or thirties and definitely single. But I've also known a few girlfriend/ boyfriend teams who have successfully worked together on ships and, assuming both partners are of a good professional standard, it can be a nice option for a couple.

Of course, the one thing you'll need more than anything else is patience with the passengers. You just have to get used to them ignoring you when you're trying to organise a series of shots and, occasionally, they can be downright rude. Gangways are often the hardest. You get sick of saying 'OK folks, let's get a picture. Stand a bit closer, next to the sign. No, this sign. That's it, now look at me...I'm over here, madam...Big smile, that's great. OK folks, let's get a picture.' You say it so many times, you repeat it in your sleep. And no matter how polite you are, there are several predictable things that passengers complain about every cruise: the weather, the air-conditioning — and the photographers. If we're always around, we get accused of pestering. If we leave them alone, they say that they can never find a photographer when they need one. Either way, we can't win. I've now resigned myself to the situation and am concerned only with the sales figures. But if, when the cruise evaluation forms come in, we rate better than the air-conditioning, then I guess it's been a good cruise.

Steven Callaghan

Technical &
Engineering

The Engineering Department covers most aspects of the ship's maintenance and workings, including the main and auxiliary engines, the gener-
ators, plumbing and sanitation, electrical systems, water desalinisation
systems, air conditioning, heating, ventilation and refrigeration.

The hub of activity is obviously the Engine Room itself. But gone are
the days of grimy stokers with sweat-drenched torsos. Computer expertise
is nowadays as important as the ability to wield a hammer, and in order
to facilitate promotion and to ensure the continuing education of their
officers, cruise lines finance college courses for engineers alongside their
work onboard (see information on training courses below).

Officers

The *Chief Engineer* (almost invariably referred to simply as 'The Chief') is in charge of this department. As the engineering equivalent of the Captain, he has a highly responsible position and is assisted by the Staff Chief Engineer (his second-in-command) and Chief Electrician.

The *Ship's Service Manager* (or similar-sounding title) is directly responsible for areas such as air conditioning, heating, refrigeration and plumbing systems. The SSM will usually be a First Engineer and, like all senior engineers, is likely to have already gained a Class I HND in Marine Engineering, otherwise known as his 'Chief's Ticket' (the engineering equivalent of a navigator's Master's Ticket). Below the rank of First Engineer are *Second, Third* and *Fourth Engineering Officers*, at appropriate stages of their training and careers.

But the journey through the ranks begins as an *Engineering Cadet*. Cadets should be between 16 and 22 years of age and are frequently recruited direct from school. Potential cadets should apply to the cruise lines for sponsorship during their final academic year and, once accepted by a company, will undergo an intensive three or four year training programme. This should combine both practical and theoretical education, leading to an HND in Marine Engineering.

The requirement for entry to the four-year course is at least five GCSE passes (preferably including physics and maths). To complete the course in three years, at least two A-level passes (including physics or maths) are needed. The first year is spent at college, the second year at sea, and the third (and fourth) year(s) back at college. For further information contact the Coordinating Agent, Merchant Navy Officer Training, Carthusian Court, 12 Carthusian St, London EC1M 6EB (tel 0171-417 8400).

Electrical Engineers pursue a similar career route, although obviously their speciality is the maintenance and repair of the ship's electrical systems. Most ships will have a *Chief, First* and *Second Electrician* and maybe several Third and Fourth Electricians. Opportunities occasionally exist for independently trained and suitably qualified electricians but they are comparatively rare.

Increasingly, opportunities also exist for *Technical Engineers* with a strong computer background (generally to degree level) and *Communications Engineers*, whose responsibilities may include the maintenance of the ship's internal telephone system (see also *A Job on the Radio* below).

All these positions assume officer status and annual salaries of approximately $20,000 (£13,500) and upwards per annum.

Ratings

Ratings (i.e. non-officer) positions do exist in the technical, engineering and electrical sectors such as *Engineering* and *Electrical Assistants, Motormen* and *Plumbers*, but cruise lines almost invariably fill such posts with workers from countries such as Indonesia or the Philippines.

Should you be lucky enough to find a company to sponsor you, you could attend a three month course for ratings at the National Sea Training College in Gravesend (address listed below). During this period you would gain instruction in ships' propulsion, auxiliary systems and machinery, with a view to becoming a Motorman.

Note, however, that as the workings of ships become increasingly sophisticated and automated, it is the jobs at the more manual end of the scale that are rapidly being reduced. The sweating 'donkeymen' with their grease-soaked vests and soot-stained neckerchiefs are nowadays seen only in old movies.

Training

Applicants for technical and engineering positions should contact the cruise lines direct or the following specialist colleges for further information. And don't forget that cargo ships and ferries also provide valuable engineering and electrical engineering opportunities at sea.

South Tyneside College, Faculty of Electrical and Electronic Engineering, St. George's Avenue, South Shields, Tyne & Wear NE34 6ET. Tel: 0191-427 3500 (ext 352).

South Tyneside College, Faculty of Marine and Mechanical Engineering, St. George's Avenue, South Shields, Tyne & Wear NE34 6ET. Tel: 0191-427 3500 (ext 402).

Southampton Institute, Maritime Operations Centre (Engineering), Warsash Campus, Newtown Road, Warsash, Hants. SO3 9ZL. Tel: 01489 576161.

Liverpool John Moores University, School of Engineering and Technology Management, Byrom St, Liverpool L3 3AF. Tel: 0151-231 2294.

Glasgow College of Nautical Studies, Department of Marine Engineering, 21 Thistle St, Glasgow G5 9XB. Tel: 0141-429 3201.

The National Sea Training College (for Ratings), Denton, Gravesend, Kent DA12 2HR. Tel: 01474 363656.

Recruitment Agencies

If you already possess relevant marine engineering, technical or electrical engineering skills and qualifications, the following employment agencies may be able to help. Note that these companies have placements for deck officers, ratings, as well as for engineers and technical assistant. Occasionally vacancies in the hotel department are also registered with them.

Trade newspapers provide information and job advertisements relating to all areas of maritime engineering. One particularly useful publication is *The Telegraph* published by NUMAST (National Union of Marine & Aviation Shipping Transport). See *Further Reading* at the end of the book for details.

A.V. Seawork Recruitment Services, Wates House, Wallington Hill, Fareham, Kent. Tel: 01489 885133.

Able Marine Services Ltd, Queen Anne's Battery, Coxside, Plymouth PL4 OLP. Tel: 01752 255007.
Crewfinders (Marine Placement Agency), 2 Markham Avenue, Sunderland SR6 7DE. Tel: 0191-529 4397.
Denholm Ltd, PO Box 200, Post Office Headquarters, Circular Rd., Douglas, Isle of Man. Tel: 01624 626582.
Humber Ship Services (Recruitment Agents), 180 High St, Hook, Nr. Goole, North Humberside, DN14 5PL. Tel: 01405 767229.
International Marine Manning Services, 4 Garland Hill, Manse Road, Belfast BT8 4YL, Northern Ireland. Tel: 01232 402759.
Marine Management Services Ltd, Celtic House, Victoria St, Douglas, Isle of Man. Tel: 01624 677776.
Sealife Crewing Services, 19-23 Canute Road, Southampton SO14 3FJ. Tel: 01703 223546.
Seamariner Ltd, Blackfield Business Centre, 114-118 Hampton Lane, Blackfield, Nr. Fawley, Southampton SO45 1WE. Tel: 01703 890432.
Seaspan Manning & Technical Services Ltd, Woodlands Annexe, 79 High St, Greenhithe, Kent DA9 9NL. Tel: 01322 387762.
SeaStaff International/Delta Marine, Personnel Services Ltd, 36 Spital Square, London E1 6DY. Tel: 0171-375 2292.
Viking Recruitment, Protea House, Marine Parade, Dover, Kent CT17 9BW. Tel: 01304 240881. For officers only.

In the Words of an Engineer

I'm a second engineer on a 70,000-ton cruise ship in the Caribbean. Maintaining such a large vessel certainly keeps us busy. No sooner do we finish at one end than we have to start again at the other. As for exercise, who needs the gym when you can walk miles just getting from deck to deck?

Needless to say, I hardly ever get off the ship. To be honest, it's not just the time, it's making the effort. When you get to my age you've been to most of the ports many times before. All I want to do when I finish work now is sit in the Ward Room (Officers' bar), have a few beers and relax.

Some of the younger guys spend a lot of time trying to keep up with technology and taking one exam after the other. You need those pieces of paper more than ever before and if I were trying to get my job all over again I probably wouldn't even be accepted. But I'm not bothered about promotion and I can live quite comfortably on my salary of $28,000 (£18,500) a year, all found.

Like the navigators, we work Watches. I'm on the eight to twelve at the moment, but often things crop up that mean we have to work well over our Watch hours. There might be a problem with the air-conditioning, for example, or a flood. We don't get many burst pipes on this particular ship, but on older vessels the plumbing can be a nightmare. I've even had to help extinguish a couple of fires in my time. I was on one ship that burnt right out due to an engine room fire that blazed out of control. We got everyone off, but it shakes you up something like that. In fact, it almost made me leave the job.

I sometimes wonder why I didn't quit. It wasn't for lack of opportunity, as engineering skills can always be used on land. I was even offered a couple of shore-based jobs around that time. Leaving the ships might have also saved my marriage. My ex-wife always wanted me to stay at home. So why didn't I? I guess it's the sea salt- it gets in the blood.

Jim MacDonald (age 54)

The Radio Room

The Radio Room is the ship's link to the outside world, and the station for all its radio, telex, telegraph, telephone and satellite communications. Although officially under the Technical & Engineering umbrella, it can be seen as something of an isolated unit in the overall workings of the ship.

In charge of this division is the *Chief Radio Officer* who, depending on the size of the vessel, may have several assistants. The day-to-day duties of the Radio Officers include urgent distress, weather and traffic communications, general ship's business (telexes, calls and faxes to and from Head Office, etc.) and the personal correspondence of passengers and crew.

As with any job of this kind, discretion and confidentiality are essential. The other current requirement is a GMDSS Certificate, which has in effect replaced the higher standard MRGC (Maritime Radio General Certificate), which included elements of Morse Code operation.

With advancements in digital communication and the demise of the Morse Code, the role of Radio Officer is rapidly changing. Many companies are even phasing out *Radio Officers* in favour of lesser-qualified agency staff *(Radio Assistants)*. But trainees still need to serve a cumulative minimum of six months at sea in order to validate their GMDSS Certificate and operate the ship's radio equipment single-handed.

Having achieved the basic GMDSS Certificate, anyone wishing to pursue a serious career in this field should aim for an HND Engineering in Electronics and Communications. This is generally a two year course, but an OND (Ordinary National Diploma) in electronics is an entry requirement that would be considered equivalent to two years of study. It is advisable to study for both OND and HND qualifications at the same establishment in order to avoid any omissions in syllabus modules.

On older vessels the plumbing can be a nightmare.

For employment in this field, together with a monthly earning potential of around $2,000 (£1,350) for agency staff and upwards of $2,500 (£1,650) for radio officers, write direct to the cruise lines or contact the independent agencies listed above (see *Recruitment Agencies*).

Training

All British colleges offering courses for Radio Officers and related personnel are affiliated to the Association of Marine Electronic Radio Colleges (AMERC). They include:

Glasgow College of Nautical Studies, Department of Telecommunications & Electronic Engineering, 21 Thistle St, Glasgow G5 9XB. Tel: 0141-429 3201.

Jewel and Esk Valley College, Milton Road Centre, 24 Milton Road East, Edinburgh EH15 2PP. Tel: 0131-660 1010.

South Tyneside College, Faculty of Electrical and Electronic Engineering, St. George's Avenue, South Shields, Tyne & Wear NE34 6ET. Tel: 0191-427 3500 (ext 352).

Southampton Institute, Marine Electronics and Communications Section, East Park Terrace, Southampton SO9 4WW. Tel: 01703 319203.
Wray Castle College, Ambleside, Cumbria LA22 OJB. Tel: 015394 32320.

Medical

Considering the hundreds or, indeed, thousands of passengers and crew on the average ship, it is hardly surprising that a reasonably equipped hospital should be a fairly standard feature. What may be surprising, however, is that sea sickness is rarely the main complaint. Medical problems of all descriptions from cardiac arrests to workplace accidents need to be swiftly treated. Although patients may later be 'landed' to shoreside hospitals, it is the members of the ship's medical team who have to cope in the interim. For this reason, a strong Accident & Emergency background is preferred for all applicants to this department.

Opportunities for Medical Staff

In charge of the Medical Department is the *Principal Medical Officer* (PMO). Depending on the size of the ship, he/she may be the only doctor, although very large vessels are more likely to have two fully-qualified *Medical Officers* (Doctors). Ships' doctors, referred to as surgeons by naval tradition, tend to be general practitioners rather than specialists (although a surprising number of Soviet gynaecologists seem to find employment on ships, especially of Greek registry, for some reason).

Most ships have a small mortuary

Doctors employed by large companies such as P & O Cruises, Princess Cruises, Cunard Line, Royal Caribbean Cruise Line, etc. and on other ships catering mainly to North American passengers, are generally licensed in the US, Canada or Great Britain. They automatically receive senior officer status, (usually three stripes) together with the appropriate salary and conditions. Depending on the cruise company, ships' doctors might also retain any treatment fees charged to passengers. Thus, the earning potential of the PMO of a busy ship's hospital could be considerably more than even the Master of the vessel.

It should be said, however, that the standard of medical services and the status given to doctors varies drastically from line to line. Some companies hire medical staff from a variety of countries and disciplines and on short-term contracts amounting to little more than a working holiday. But some (notably, US) medical organisations, such as the American College of Emergency Physicians, are becoming increasingly aware of the special demands of shipboard medical practices and now operate specific divisions in cruise medicine.

In most cases ships' doctors are assisted by a team which may include nurses, physiotherapists, etc. Qualified and experienced *Nurses* (RGN or equivalent), preferably with a strong Accident & Emergency or Intensive Care background, are needed. Many ships employ only one nurse, but some vessels may require two or more onboard at any time, including a *Senior Nurse*. Nurses generally receive two-stripe officer status and a salary of $20,000 (£13,500) and upwards per year.

One, two or three *Medical Orderlies* with appropriate training and experience are also employed on most ships, depending on the size. Medical orderlies usually have Petty Officer status and an accompanying annual salary of $10,000 (£6,500) and upwards.

On smaller vessels, the nurse and/or orderly may also act as dispenser, whereas larger ships may employ a qualified *Medical Dispenser* (also a Petty Officer) on a full-time basis.

Two other positions found only on larger vessels are those of a qualified and experienced *Physiotherapist* and *Dentist*. On most ships the doctor will administer emergency treatment or pain-killers until a suitable appointment can be made for the passenger or crew member to consult a shoreside dentist or physiotherapist. Only on larger ships (and even then, only on longer cruises) can the luxury of an onboard dentist or physio be accommodated, which is why these professionals tend to work at sea for just several months of the year, to supplement their work on land.

Anyone in a position to apply for any of these medical positions, should contact the cruise lines direct, and compare contract terms.

In the Words of a Nurse

I am employed as a nurse onboard a cruise ship currently sailing the Indian Ocean. I have worked on six different ships over the past seven years, and each ship has been quite different in terms of the medical facilities it offers. These range from the well-equipped hospital with full operating theatre and isolation units to basic sick bays without even an X-ray machine. This means you really have to be quite adaptable. An ability to cope (or at least appear to cope) is an important asset, especially in what for a land-based nurse may be difficult or unusual circumstances. Rough seas, for example, can affect your duties, even though the hospital will be situated in the most stable part of the ship (towards the middle of a lower deck). Working conditions may be more cramped than is usual onshore; and you are frequently faced with medical decisions that would not be expected of a nurse in a shoreside hospital.

The amount of responsibility I had was the hardest factor for me to accept when I first started working at sea. Even with a strong background in Intensive Care and Accident & Emergency, I was simply not used to being the only trained person around when a medical emergency arose. Here, outside the surgery hours (which we work together), the doctor and I work an alternating duty rota that includes days in port. This means he could be ashore at the very time the carpenter cuts an artery or a passenger has a coronary. And I then have to deal with the situation single-handed.

We operate surgery hours with different times for passengers and crew, although we may also be called out at all times of the day or night to deal with an emergency and annoyingly, non-emergency, cases. That's the thing with this job. You never know what tomorrow will bring. You can be having an easy cruise when, all of a sudden, someone needs intensive care and your working hours are suddenly doubled.

Of course, if the patient is dangerously ill or in need of a major operation, the doctor may decide to land them to an onshore hospital. I've known several occasions when the ship has actually changed course and altered its itinerary because of such emergencies. But naturally, considerations such as the medical standards and facilities of the country in question are taken into account. It would usually be crazy, for example, to get the ship's agents to deal with all the arrangements and legislation of landing a patient in Alexandria if the very next day the ship is due to call at Haifa.

On this subject, I'm always asked if we get many deaths on board and whether or not we have a mortuary. Naturally, with so many passengers and crew members, especially in view of the age group of many of the passengers, occasional deaths are inevitable. When they occur, however, the situation can be more traumatic for the bereaved than if it were onshore because of the unfamiliar environment. One of the hardest aspects of my job is trying to give comfort to some elderly lady, who has probably never before ventured out of Sutton Coldfield and is unexpectedly widowed on her first cruise. To see her, now faced with the prospect of being landed in, say, Mombasa with her hastily-packed cases and the body of her late husband, is heart-rending, to say the least. But, beyond sympathy, all you can do is hope the ship's agents will help her through the formalities.

Burials at sea are very uncommon nowadays because of the need for a coroner's report, and the majority of corpses are flown home for burial. Most ships have a small mortuary, situated in or near the hospital, although I did work on one vessel where lack of space meant a body was kept in a refrigerated cheese store.

Needlesss to say, the crew demand for Danish Blue hit an all-time low that week.

Apart from the job itself, which can be very rewarding, I especially enjoy the travel aspect of working on cruise ships. I have a particular interest in archaeology, so to visit places such as Chichen Itza, Giza, Ephesus and Olympia is a great bonus for me.

On the down side, ours can be a sexist department where male doctors are frequently employed in preference to female and female nurses in preference to male. Also, promotion prospects are nil. You come in as a nurse, you go out as a nurse. I have considered returning to nursing on shore, but I think I would find it boring now. On land, I might work in Outpatients, Surgical Unit, Intensive Care Unit or Accident & Emergency department. At sea, I work in all of them at the same time!

Carole Henderson (age 35)

Which Ship?

We have now considered the huge range of opportunities for employment provided by various departments of a cruise ship. But each cruise line and every ship is different, and it is worth becoming acquainted with some of these differences.

To the puzzled job-seeker thumbing through a handful of cruise brochures, the seven seas may seem truly unfathomable, such are the choices available. Add to this the frequent changes in the industry — not to mention numerous ships and companies with confusingly similar names — and one may easily feel swamped by possibilities.

Whether you go for the theory that 'biggest is best' or prefer the approachability of a smaller line; whether you like the aristocratic or the more plebeian lines, you will want to be assured that you have found the most suitable conditions and the best deal for your particular skills.

MAJOR CRUISE LINES

The following descriptions of cruise lines and vessels may help to distinguish between them. Addresses are all in the list of *Cruise Line Addresses* below. Further information is included in the section *Who Owns the Ships?*

Cunard

At the long-established, traditional end of the cruising industry, **Cunard Line** operates a diverse fleet, ranging from the sophisticated yacht-like *Sea Goddesses* to the friendly, informal *Cunard Countess* (with arguably the best itinerary in the Caribbean). Including its famous flagship the *Queen Elizabeth 2*, Cunard currently owns six out of the ten top-rated ships in the world, according to the independent surveys of the MEG (Maritime Evaluations Group). Having recently acquired the prestigious *Royal Viking Sun*, Cunard now seems set on securing the upper echelons of the cruising market and is currently the only company to have three ships offering a World Cruise, namely the *QE2*, the *Sagafjord* and *Royal Viking Sun*. Whether the situation will change now that the parent company Trafalgar House has been sold to the Norwegian company Kvaerner (March 1996) remains to be seen, though it would appear that the future of even the *QE2* is in some doubt.

But at least for the present, the *QE2* is still the most famous vessel sailing the high seas, despite the disastrous publicity concerning her recent refurbishment and competition from all those new, glitzy super-ships. Ports as far removed as Liverpool, Hong Kong and Auckland reserve a special welcome for 'The Queen', and in Japan she is, quite simply, a superstar. Kieran Lynch, a 25 year old barman from Dublin, describes the ship's recent departure from the port of Kagoshima:

We didn't sail until late in the evening and I remember hundreds if not thousands of local people descending on the harbour to watch us leave. They were all clammering for souvenirs, and passengers were throwing postcards and beermats down to them from the open decks. It was like something out of an old black-and-white movie. As we pulled away from the quayside, the ship sounded its horn and 'Auld Lang Syne' started to play through the port loudspeakers. By then it was quite dark and all those on the dockside were waving little Chinese lanterns that lit up the night. Even when we were way out to sea, you could still make out those bobbing orange lights. There are so many special events during the World Cruise, but the highlight is the 'Queen' herself.

Critics of the line say that the company is too keen to cling to its traditions and places undue emphasis on pandering to its ever decreasing (because ever-deceasing) clique of regular passengers. But in terms of cruise line pedigree, the company that once sailed the *Queen Mary* is still very much a leader of the pack.

Other Deluxe Lines

Of course, if working on a really deluxe cruise ship is your specific aim, you should definitely consider applying to **Crystal Cruises**, owners of the magnificent *Crystal Harmony* and her new sister ship the *Crystal Symphony*. These vessels epitomise the changes that have taken place in passenger ship design over recent years. Once aboard, within sight of the waterfall (no less) in the spacious lobby, you could be excused for thinking you were not afloat at all, but rather in an elegant five star hotel.

Two other major contenders in the top price bracket were the **Holland America** and **Royal Viking** lines. It is interesting to note, however, that both have suffered upheavals in recent times. Holland America Line is now owned by the Carnival Corporation, while Royal Viking's once-impressive fleet had dwindled to two ships by 1994, when the *Royal Viking Sun* was purchased by Cunard, who combined their names to create the *Cunard Royal Viking*.

Carnival

In the light of these changes, one might be tempted to surmise that the big profits are no longer to be made at the pricey end of the market. **Carnival Cruise Lines**, with its flagrantly successful 'supermarket' approach, is floating proof of this. Yet the Carnival Corporation which owns Carnival Cruise Lines has staked a larger claim on the upper regions of the market than many people are aware. It now owns not only the prestigious Holland America Line but also the luxurious smaller vessels of **Seabourn Cruise Line**, the elegant sailing yachts of **Windstar Cruises** and the recently-acquired fleet of the well-established **Norwegian Cruise Line (NCL)**. Quite a catch for the 'Safeways' of the industry.

Love it or loathe it, Carnival also leads the way in cruising's design revolution. Unashamedly brash, this is Las Vegas at sea, complete with fake Egyptian mummies, life-size model elephants, fire-breathing Chinese dragons and psychedelic neon. Just as many people go to Las Vegas to see Caesar's Palace rather than to gamble in it, so passengers are booking cruises on Carnival ships for the ship itself. From the tip of those 'whale-tail' funnels to the outrageous themed decor within, this type of escapist vacation may represent the future of cruising.

Carnival make no bones about the fact that they are aiming for the young first-time cruiser rather than trying to cultivate a more discerning clientele who will return for many more cruises. But this youthful exuberance suits many people and if you are looking to work hard and play hard, then this could be the company for you. As for sun, sea, sand and sex, it can only be assumed that these are perks of the job in a workplace called *Ecstasy, Fantasy* or *Sensation*.

Disney

Carnival's future rival in the 'theme park at sea' stakes could well be none other than the very company that leads the world in theme parks on land, the giant Disney Corporation. The recently-formed **Disney Cruise Lines** are due to launch their first two ships in 1998, with itineraries out of Port Canaveral in Florida, and package deals to include stays at the Disney World Resort and Disney's private island. Needless to say, there will be plenty of employment opportunities on these mammoth 85,000 GRT vessels (gross registered tonnage) for early-bird job-seekers. Children's counsellors and would-be Mickeys, Minnies and Plutos take note.

Tails may be worn in the evening

P & O

The former Peninsular & Oriental Steam Navigation Company and now P & O Cruises is a long-standing British company, appealing to predominantly British passengers. Like Cunard, P & O boasts an enviable pedigree that dates back to the early 1800s and, like Cunard, is a good source of employment for British officers and staff.

Together with the affiliated fleets of P & O Holidays, P & O Spice Island Cruises, Swan Hellenic Cruises and P & O European Ferries, this line operates a diverse range of ships. But the *Canberra,* affectionately dubbed 'the Great White Whale' and once P & O's rival to the QE2, is now something of an old lady and likely to be superseded by their new 'megaship', the *Oriana.*

The larger, more 'American' division of the P & O Group, **Princess Cruises**, is the company forever associated with *The Love Boat,* the television series originally filmed on the *Pacific Princess* which sold the romance of cruising to millions of viewers in almost a hundred countries. The programme may have ceased production and the fleet upgraded to include the distinctive dolphin-shaped *Crown Princess, Regal Princess* and the mammoth new *Sun Princess.* But the publicity brochures ensure that the *Love Boat* association lives on. They too use British officers, as well as Italian and Scandinavian ones.

RCCL

If cruising to you means the Caribbean, then consider applying to **Royal Caribbean Cruise Line (RCCL)**. In keeping with its name, this company bases the majority of its ships in West Indian waters for at least part of the year. Their large well-equipped vessels (the *Legend of the Seas* and *Splendour of the Seas* even boast an 18-hole golf course) offer plenty of employment opportunities in all sectors of the industry. Each ship displays the company's distinctive blue anchor logo as part of an easily identifiable corporate image that attracts a faithful, predominantly American, following of passengers.

OTHER LINES

European Cruise Lines

European passengers are more likely to be found on the ships of the successful Italian company, **Costa Cruise Lines (Costa Crociere)**. Linguistic skills — and the ability to make very loud announcements in five languages throughout the day — are a definite advantage for job-seekers with this company. Costa may not win any prizes when it comes to ship beauty contests but potential cruise staff might have fun at all those toga parties.

The frequently-chartered ships of **Epirotiki Lines** and **Black Sea Shipping** also provide numerous opportunities for linguistically-talented Europeans. The former is a traditional Greek company (now sailing under the umbrella of **Royal Olympic Cruises**); the latter, Ukrainian. But bear in mind that both fleets comprise predominantly older vessels that lack the glitz of some of their more modern counterparts.

Sprechen Sie Deutsch? German-speaking job-seekers will be interested to learn that the ships of Black Sea Shipping and other East European companies are often chartered by German cruise operators such as Transocean Reederei, Seetours International, Hanseatic Tours, Phoenix Reisen, Neckermann Seereisen and Deutsche Seereederei. The latter is an especially good bet since it is due to launch two brand new ships of its own *(Aida* and *Aida II)* in 1997. Non-German-speaking North American applicants, on the other hand, may do better to contact the US charterer, the **OdessAmerica Cruise Company.**

The main claim to fame of the **Norwegian Cruise Line (NCL)** is that it owns what was at one time the world's largest cruise ship, the 76,049-ton *SS Norway* (formerly *The France*). Its other five vessels, however, are more moderately sized and identifiable by their names ending in 'ward': *Dreamward, Seaward,* and so on. Before its takeover by the Carnival Corporation, NCL used to shelter under the overall umbrella of the **Kloster Cruise Company**, which also housed **Royal Cruise Line (RCL)**, a fleet of ships, each ending in 'Odyssey'. It has been learned at the time of writing that NCL has subsumed the Royal Cruise Line, retaining two of its ships and selling the other two.

Theme Cruises

Ships which offer theme cruises may provide specialist employment opportunities, especially for classical, jazz, big band and Country & Western musicians. Two particularly high-profile music cruises are the annual Classical Music Festival aboard the *Mermoz* (Paquet French Cruises) and the annual Floating Jazz Festival on the *Norway* (NCL).

Independent charterers like Classical Cruises may specialise in themes like archaeology, horticulture (particularly popular on Madeira/Canary Islands itineraries), cookery, wine tasting and murder mystery.

HOW OLD?

New Ships

The parent company of **Chandris Cruises** houses two cruise lines, **Celebrity** and **Fantasy Cruises,** both with predominantly Greek officers and an international staff and crew. For prospects of work, Chandris may be a particularly good bet. Two new 'superships' (the *Galaxy* and *Constellation*) are due to be launched under the Celebrity flag by the year 2000, following hot on the keel of the appropriately-named *Century*.

In the race to build new ships, the other leaders of the pack are Carnival Cruise Lines with six new mega-ships in the pipeline, Royal Caribbean Cruise Line with five (including the 73,000 ton sister ships, *Grandeur of the Seas* and *Enchantment of the Seas*), Holland America Line (the *New Rotterdam*) and Princess Cruises (the *Dawn Princess* and *Grand Princess*). Disney Cruise Lines is also likely to be an innovative name in the future of the industry, together with **Star Cruise,** a Malaysian company in the process of building two more ships for a 1998 launch, the *SuperStar Leo* and *SuperStar Virgo*.

Interestingly enough, the one thing that all of these yet-to-be-launched ships have in common is their massive size. Carnival Cruise Lines' *Destiny* and Princess Cruises' *Grand Princess* are expected to tip the scales at 100,000 and 105,000 tons respectively, which will easily break the record. At present the world's largest cruise ship is the *Sun Princess*, with a gross registered tonnage of 77,000 tons. Within a few years there

New ships can have drawbacks

will be at least a dozen ships larger than the *QE2* at 70,000 tons, which will create a few problems. For example in its bid to steal the title of World's Biggest Ship, the *Grand Princess* will be too large to pass through the Panama Canal.

Of course, to the traditionalist, the environmentalist, and even the experienced cruiser, the new ships are no better than floating apartment blocks with their deckless sides and high-rise sterns to maximise cabin space. Some consider them nothing but ugly, polluting, impractical blots on the horizon. However to the job-seeker, they're very good news indeed.

Older Ships

In contrast to what some regard as 'modern monstrosities,' many European vessels (especially Greek and Ukrainian-registered ships) are well into middle-age and possibly almost pensionable. But there can be advantages to working on an older vessel. Wine steward, Georgiou Andropoulos, explains:

> *I have worked on seven different ships for three different companies, and I can honestly say I prefer the older ones. Sure, the newer ships are glitzier and easier to keep clean but they don't have the atmosphere that an old ship has. Atmosphere is like a good claret, it takes time to develop and mature. I know many*

people who would rather work on a 'tub' with a good atmosphere than a new ship straight from the yard. If a ship is new, so is the crew, and because people may be trying to prove themselves, they tend to enforce more rules and regulations. Plus, there are bound to be teething problems. 'Shake-down' trips and maiden voyages are invariably cruises from hell.

In terms of facilities, there may be more space for the passengers on a new ship but crew cabins are often small and you just don't get the craftsmanship that you did even 20 years ago. Neither can they take the weather. Because of their shallower draft, the slightest swell and they roll all over the place (seasickness sufferers take note). Older ships were built to last. It is hard to imagine any of today's megaships still working in the year 2050.

While taking into account Georgiou's enthusiasm for ships of character, one should also consider the viewpoint of senior engineer, Eddie McKenzie:

Of course older ships have character. They are also more likely to have plumbing, sanitation and air-conditioning problems, together with difficulty in complying with modern fire and safety regulations. Many of the ferries and 'tubs' floating around the Mediterranean barely meet the standards set by the IMO and might well not pass a standard US Coastguard inspection. From a servicing point of view, give me a new ship any day!

HOW BIG?

Apart from the age of a vessel, the most important factor for the nautical job-seeker to bear in mind is size, because the size of a ship can make a huge difference to the working and social conditions.

Large Ships

Larger ships with as many as 2,000 passengers and 1,000 crew members obviously offer wider social possibilities and greater earning potential for those relying on tips. There may also be better crew facilities, including sports and leisure programmes. On the downside, large ships are more likely to have to anchor (rather than dock) at the various ports of call and the use of tenders can severely restrict crew shore leave since passengers always have priority). By their very nature, large ships are bound to be more impersonal and you will be lucky to get to know even a third of the crew. They also tend to enforce more regulations. But if you are outgoing, independent and like the anonymity that working in a large workplace affords, you will want to consider Costa Cruise Lines, Princess Cruises, Carnival Cruise Lines, Crystal Cruises, Holland America Line and Royal Caribbean Cruise Line.

Another possible advantage of the very large ships is that they often control operations in the staff sector (production shows, casino, beauty salon, fitness and gift shops) that would be delegated to a concessionaire by smaller ships.

Small Ships

Very small ships with less than 200 passengers and 100 crew members have advantages such as their ability to dock alongside in virtually every port and to follow unusual itineraries inaccessible to bigger ships. Naturally there will be a much more intimate atmosphere on board. On the down side, there may be fewer (if any) facilities for the crew. On the one hand, you will get to know your colleagues better. On the other, they will get to know your business better, and gossip on any ship is rife.

Small ships have a more intimate atmosphere

The other major factor about working on a very small ship is that the nature of your job may differ drastically from the same position on a larger vessel. Versatility tends to be the key and it is not unusual to find the Hotel Manager directing housekeeping or the Cruise Director acting as concierge. The programme of activities may be quite different or even non-existent. This tends to happen at the 'mega money' end of the market, where passengers virtually dictate what they wish to do and when. There may even be scope for the passengers to suggest the route the ship takes. In these cases the ambience onboard may be more akin to a private yacht than a cruise ship, with the emphasis on water sports and top-class dining. Very few opportunities therefore exist in the field of entertainment, other than for musicians to play dance music and pianists with a cocktail and classical repertoire.

If you prefer a more intimate workplace off the usual tourist track and think you can cope with a wealthier and potentially more demanding clientele, apply to Cunard Line (*Sea Goddess I and II*), Seabourn Cruise Line (*Seabourn Pride* and *Seabourn Spirit*), **Renaissance Cruises** with eight ships, **Radisson Seven Seas Cruises** (*Radisson Diamond* and *Song of Flower*) and **Silversea Cruises** (*Silver Cloud* and *Silver Wind*).

Note also that smaller vessels naturally tend to be less stable in rough seas than their bigger counterparts. If you are prone to sea-sickness, it may be best to try working on a larger ship first.

Mid-Size Ships

Somewhere between the giants and the terribly exclusive lies the vast mid-range of ships catering to the vast mid-range of passengers. For many cruise ship employees, vessels which carry between 400 and 1,200 passengers and between 200 and 600 crew members provide the best of both worlds. They are big enough to offer reasonable facilities yet sufficiently small to be friendly and able to dock in many of their ports of call.

Companies with a good range of mid-sized ships are mainly described above, including the P & O Group, Royal Caribbean Cruise Line, Black Sea Shipping (frequently chartered by companies like CTC Cruises and Transocean Reederei), Chandris Cruises, Costa Cruise Lines, Cunard Line, Epirotiki/Sun Line Cruises (marketed under Royal Olympic Cruises), Louis Cruise Line of Cyprus and Norwegian Cruise Line (NCL).

SAILING SHIPS & YACHTS

Those with a taste for adventure might like to consider ships with sails. Unfortunately their relatively small passenger carry means that yachts and sail-ships do not offer an abundance of work opportunities. Many chartered yachts are hired to experienced sailors as 'bareboats' (i.e. with no crew provided) and even larger sailing vessels may use less than a dozen crew members. With the exception of the Windstar and Club Med ships mentioned below, there are usually no casinos or spa/gymnasium facilities onboard vessels with sails and very few jobs for musicians and entertainers. The opportunities that do exist are particularly good for experienced captains and qualified chefs. But bear in mind that vessels registered in the United States are crewed by Americans or US work permit holders only.

Club Mediterranée has the world's largest sail-cruisers (*Club Med I and II*) while the oldest and possibly the most prestigious is **Sea Cloud's** beautiful ship of the same name (see **Deilmann Reederei** in list of *Cruise Lines & Operators*).

Windstar Cruises have three sail-cruise ships (*Wind Song, Wind Spirit* and *Wind Star*), **Star Clippers** have two (*Star Clipper* and *Star Flyer*), **Tall Ship Adventures** own the *Sir Francis Drake,* and French-speaking applicants might even get to scale the rigging for the **Compagnie des Isles du Ponant** on their vessel *Le Ponant*.

Le Ponant is represented in the United States by Worldwide Travel & Cruise Associates, which also markets several sailing vessels including catamarans on Australia's Great Barrier Reef. **Zeus Cruises** operates motor-sailers/yachts around the most charming and least visited ports of the Aegean. Deilmann Reederei brings a German flavour to the Caribbean and Baltic with the beautiful schooner, *Lili Marleen*. **Dirigo Cruises** has 16 sailing ships, mainly located in the South Seas. **Nautical Resources, Inc** has three elegant sailing ships with itineraries that include the Panama Canal. **Maine Windjammers** operates three ships out of Rockland, Maine, while **Windjammer Barefoot Cruises** in Maimi employs approximately 300 people to cater to the needs of the 30,000 passengers it carries annually on its six vessel-fleet throughout the Caribbean. The largest yacht chartering and management company in the world is **The Moorings** with a fleet of almost 700 vessels, although **Sacks Yacht Charters** also operates sail and motor vessels around the globe. All of the above companies are listed in the alphabetical list of addresses at the end of the book.

Yacht Crewing Agencies

Those seeking work specifically on yachts or sailing vessels might wish to consider enlisting the help of a crewing agency, some of which charge an annual subscription of about £30:

Blue Water Yacht Crew Agency, La Galerie du Port, 8 Boulevard d'Aguillon, 06600 Antibes, France. Tel: 93 34 34 13.

Crewit, Shute Hill Cottage, Marlborough, Kingsbridge, Devon TQ7 3SG. Tel: 01548 561897.

Crew Placement, 1550 SE 17th St, Fort Lauderdale, FL 33316, USA. Tel: 305-763-1841.

Crew Search International, 17 Gillingham St, London SW1, England. Tel: 01572 477906.

Crewseekers, Hawthorn House, Hawthorn Lane, Sarisbury Green, Southampton SO1 7BD. Tel: 01489 578319. Claim to be the largest crewing agency in Europe.

The Cruising Association, CA House, 1 Northey St, Limehouse Basin, London E14 8BT. Tel: 0171-537 2828.

Peter Insull's Yacht Crew Agency, La Galerie du Port, 8 Boulevard d'Aguillon, 06600 Antibes, France. Tel: 93 34 64 64.

Sea Gem International, Rectory Road, Broadstairs, Kent CT10 1HG. Tel: 01843 867960.

Travelmate, 52 York Place, Bournemouth BH7 6JN. Tel: 01202 431520.

Look in trade magazines such as *Yachting World, Yachting Monthly* and *Yachts & Yachting* for related information on yachting schools, clubs and associations, brokers and charter companies. It may also be useful to contact the Royal Yachting Association (RYA House, Romsey Road, Eastleigh, Hants. SO50 9YA; 01703 629962) and the Yacht

Charter Association (60 Silverdale, New Milton, Hants. BH25 7DE; 01425 610967).

CRUISING ITINERARIES

Most of the major players have ships around the globe, while smaller lines may concentrate on one region. Naturally, you will want to bear in mind the itineraries of a company's fleet before applying to them. This way, you can avoid accepting a contract for the Mexican Riviera when you can't stand the heat or a series of Atlantic crossings when you go green on the Mersey Ferry.

The routes of specific vessels can be found in the chapter *Facts About the Ships.* As a general guide, the main cruising areas, together with their respective advantages and disadvantages, are as follows:

Transatlantic Crossings

It is surprising how few transatlantic crossings there are any more. Apart from ships navigating the South Atlantic as part of a broader itinerary (from Europe to the Caribbean via Madeira and the Canary Islands, for example), only the *QE2* offers a regular route across the Atlantic. The fact that she is the best (some say, the only) ship currently suited to this passage does not detract from the monotony of five grey days at sea and frequently heavy swells. And forget the idea of time off in New York or Southampton. No sooner do you reach your destination than you turn straight round and do the whole thing over again. On the bright side, sailing past Liberty Island is the most exciting way to enter Manhattan. And you will save money, since there are no ports of call in which to spend it.

Around the World

Circumnavigating the world, on the other hand, is a much brighter prospect, and it may be worth suffering the *QE2* 'ferry service' to stake your claim on the world cruise. Although the 'Queen' offers the most prestigious round-the-world tour, several other ships do extended cruises, including the *Royal Viking Sun* and *Sagafjord* (Cunard Line), the *Rotterdam* and *Statendam* (Holland America Line), the *Oriana* (P & O Cruises), the *Europa* (Hapag Lloyd Cruises), the *Asuka* (NYK Cruises), the *Maxim Gorki* (under charter to Phoenix Reisen), the *Royal Odyssey* (Norwegian Cruise Line) and several of Black Sea Shipping's vessels under charter to various operators.

Most world cruises start in January and last approximately three months, which sounds an exciting prospect. But there is a down side: lots of hard-working sea days without a break for a start–you will be lucky to get off in even a third of the ports–and the frequently low (even half empty) passenger carry is not conducive to high earnings.

There is a popular theory at sea: the more expensive the cruise, the older the clientele. Judging from the large number of walking frames parked outside guest accommodation on round-the-world cruises, it may be true. But there are no prizes for witty staff members who, when asked the average age of the passengers, promptly answer 'deceased'.

Taking into account the fact that global itineraries can become predictable, some crew members actually turn down repeat offers ('Ho, hum, not another World Cruise') in favour of shorter passages on other ships. But for the first-timer, to go around the world in 80 (more commonly 90) days is an experience that no would-be traveller should miss.

Caribbean

Traditionally the preferred destination of beach lovers, short-stay passengers and scuba divers, the West Indies are not always the most popular with cruise ship employees who find that the region can become boring on long contracts. Most of the cruises sail out of Miami, including a host of three and four-day 'cheapies.' Anyone who happens to play in a steel/calypso band and others who want to earn a high commission from the onshore duty-free shops will want to concentrate on this itinerary. A disincentive is the fact that both recent hurricanes and long-term tourist exploitation have left their scars. For example the island of St. Maarten sometimes resembles a cruise ship parking lot. But those balmy Caribbean nights can still be wonderfully romantic (except, possibly, in San Juan where you are likely to witness a shooting rather than a shooting star).

Most of the major lines have itineraries which include the Caribbean. Try especially Carnival Cruise Lines, Celebrity Cruises, Clipper Cruise Line, Costa Cruise Lines, Cunard Line, Dolphin Cruise Line, Holland America Line, New Commodore Cruise Line, Norwegian Cruise Line, Princess Cruises, Royal Caribbean Cruise Line, Star Clippers and Special Expeditions.

Alaska

The standard route covers the west coast of North America between Vancouver and Seward (the port for Anchorage). Again, this itinerary soon becomes boring on a long contract. Wildlife spotters may enjoy this run, the scenery is magnificent and it is certainly good to breathe fresher air (not relevant if you work in the engine room) but be prepared for inclement (rather than simply cold) weather. Many crew members become ten pin bowling experts during this contract.

Cruising in Alaska is very much dominated by Princess Cruises, as they also have a large shoreside travel operation here. Holland America Line with its affiliated travel operation, Westours is also a good bet for work in Alaska, while **Special Expeditions** and **World Explorer Cruises** may appeal to hardier individuals. Cunard Line could be worth a try since its *Crown Dynasty* spends the summer months here. American job-seekers might like to contact **Alaska Sightseeing/Cruise West,** since this US-registered company has several small coastal vessels in these waters.

Mediterranean

The Mediterranean Sea provides scope for much more variety than most itineraries. From the Greek islands to the French Riviera, the Pyramids to the Colosseum, the Med has everything a seafaring person could want: sun, sand, good food, fine wine, ancient history, gay bars and telephones that work. Beware of contracts leaving from Tilbury or Southampton though. The convenience of home ports (for the British) is really no match for being thrown around the Bay of Biscay (even on a good day).

Numerous companies operate ships for those wishing to head for the Med, including: Airtours Cruises, Black Sea Shipping, CTC Cruise Lines, Club Med, Costa Cruise Lines, Cunard Line, Fantasy Cruises, Fred Olsen Cruises, Intercruise, Louis Cruise Lines, Majestic International Cruises, P & O Cruises, Paquet French Cruises, Paradise Cruises, Radisson Seven Seas Cruises, Renaissance Cruises, Royal Olympic Cruises (incorporating Epirotiki Lines and Sun Line Cruises), Seabourn Cruise Line and Starlauro Cruises. (All addresses in list at end of book.)

Scandinavia and the Baltic

The weather's too cold and the guests are too old for the 'Kiss-Me-Quick' Romeos of other itineraries. Rather, this is more of a cultural route with clean cities, fresh air and folkloric dancers waving handkerchiefs. Midnight Sun seekers tend to be richer than regular sun-seekers, so tips are good. If you intend eating or drinking ashore, you'll have to earn a lot of extra in tips, as prices are so high.

Baltic Line, Black Sea Shipping and its charterers, CTC Cruise Lines, Costa Cruise Lines, Cunard Line, Festival Cruises, P & O Cruises, Seabourn Cruise Line and Silversea Cruises may be of particular interest to those wishing to work in these waters. Also, Bergen Line operate a fleet of passenger/cargo vessels (address in *Cargo & Ferry Companies*) in the coastal areas of Norway and the Arctic Circle.

Black Sea

Often combined with cruises in the Eastern Mediterranean, this route offers more folkloric dancers waving handkerchiefs (or could they be the same ones in different boots?). It also offers the cultural experience of a matinée at the opera, bargain massage and tin of fake caviar. For work opportunities, check out the cruise lines that operate ships in the Mediterranean as several of them also include the Black Sea in their summer itineraries.

Far East and Indian Ocean

Most opportunities to discover the mysteries of the East seem to occur as part of a more general itinerary, such as a World Cruise. Find yourself on a Slow Boat to China and you could also pick up bargains in Bali,

Hong Kong and Thailand. There are some notable exceptions however, such as the *Pacific Princess, Renaissance VI* and *Sea Goddess II* (all of which use Singapore as a base port for their itineraries in Asian waters at least for part of the year). The seamier 'gambling and prostitution' ships which sail out of Singapore are probably best avoided.

The current batch of Orient-based cruise lines are mainly one-ship operations, too numerous to list and catering primarily to the Asian passenger market. But many shipping executives believe that as the Caribbean reaches saturation point the Far East could become the popular cruising destination of the future for all the major lines. In the meantime, however, try Crystal Cruises, Cunard Line, Orient Lines, Princess Cruises, Radisson Seven Seas Cruises, Renaissance Cruises, Seabourn Cruise Line, Star Cruise, Star Line Cruises (note that the Royal Star offers interesting cruise-safari packages in the South Indian Ocean) and Windstar Cruises. Japanese-speakers should also try Mitsui OSK Passenger Line and NYK Cruises.

Hawaii and the South Pacific

Sail in the wake of Captains Cook and Bligh to find sparkling seas, picture postcard beaches and the real Bali Ha'i. Discover fire walkers in Fiji and fire water in Tahiti (called *kava*), be a beach bum on Waikiki, and trade those boring luncheon vouchers for a barbecue in beautiful Bora Bora. Somebody's got to do it.

If you'd like that somebody to be you, try P & O Spice Island Cruises (part of the P & O Group, incorporating several small island-hopping vessels), expedition companies such as Abercrombie & Kent, Noble Caledonia, Quark and Special Expeditions, and smaller upmarket companies such as Seabourn Cruise Line, Radisson Seven Seas Cruises, Club Med, Renaissance and Windstar Cruises). Note that the appropriately named American Hawaii Cruises may be a good bet for US citizens, but their American registry excludes most European applicants.

Great Barrier Reef

To work your passage downunder to Australia and New Zealand, try Cunard Line, Holland America Line, P & O Cruises, Princess Cruises, Radisson Seven Seas Cruises, Seabourn Cruise Line and Worldwide Travel & Cruise Associates.

Bahamas/Bermuda

Often included in Caribbean itineraries and short Miami special offers, the Bahamas offer sun, sand and the chance to stock up on basic provisions, such as bags of tortilla chips and shaving foam. This is also a good place to deal with British passport/C1-D Visa formalities. Bermuda serves the same purpose on different itineraries. (But be warned of Bermuda's hidden danger–not the Triangle but a crash course (literally) in moped riding. Tragically, too many crew members survive one but not the other.

Carnival, Dolphin, Majesty, Norwegian, Premier and Royal Caribbean Cruise Lines all operate short cruises in the Bahamas. Celebrity and Regal Cruises, Majesty, Norwegian and Royal Caribbean Cruise Line also operate 7-day cruises out of Bermuda.

Central and South America

If you like nightlife, this is the route for you. Acapulco, Buenos Aires, Rio de Janeiro are exciting, sensual cities, which satisfy even the wildest night owl. As for bargain hunters, you can buy all your souvenirs here and still have enough to feed the throng of vagrants who will be following you around. Calling the folks back home could be a problem, as can calling for help, should you inadvertently stray into an undesirable neighbourhood. It has to be said, these ports can be dangerous. True, the best view of Rio is seen when entering from the sea, but that's not the reason why people choose to stay onboard.

The cruise lines to try include Carnival Cruise Lines, Crystal Cruises, Cunard Line, Holland America Line, Norwegian Cruise Line, Princess Cruises, Royal Caribbean Cruise Line and Special Expeditions. The vessels of several of these companies also include the Panama Canal in their itineraries.

Rivers

Of course, a cruise doesn't have to be at sea. There are numerous passenger vessels offering opportunities on rivers on all the continents. The river boats of **Amazon Tours & Cruises** and smaller cruise ships such as the *Pacific Princess* may follow the mighty Amazon. The **Delta Queen Steamboat Company** (also owners of **American Hawaii Cruises**) operates paddle steamers on the Mississippi River. The **American West Steamboat Company** runs its first vessel out of Portland; and **St. Lawrence Cruise Lines** and the **American Canadian Caribbean Line** offer cruises along the coastline and inland waterways of Canada and the Americas. Note, however, that US registered vessels employ only US citizens/work permit holders.

With the increasing popularity of China as a tourist destination, companies such as **Abercrombie & Kent** (for **Regal China Cruises**), **Victoria Cruises** and the **China Yangtze River Shipping Company** all operate riverboats along the meandering 3,500 miles of the Yangtze River. **Orient Express Cruises** have recently set up an unusual itinerary in Myanmar (formerly Burma) between Mandalay and Pagan on their appropriately-named deluxe river cruiser *Road to Mandalay.*

Approximately 150 vessels cruise the River Nile; most are operated by local companies or hotel groups including Sonnesta Hotels and Hilton, Sheraton and Oberoi Nile Cruises, although Abercrombie & Kent also has three boats in Egypt.

As for Europe, Abercrombie & Kent offers chartered barge trips throughout England, France and the Netherlands. The American operator, Eurocruises, markets more than 70 boats and ships, including many East European vessels; and the KD German Rhine Line and Peter Deilmann Shipping (Deilmann Reederei, marketed by Cunard Europamerica River Cruises, a division of the Cunard Line) covers the Danube, Rhone, Elbe, Moselle and many other rivers.

Note, however, that many river vessels are chartered or marketed by one organisation for another and that such operators are rarely involved in hiring staff. In many cases, the local workforce can supply a full complement of staff. The range of available jobs is sometimes so limited that, unless you are a specialist lecturer or a very bad sailor, you may do better to send your CV/resumé elsewhere.

Britain

Although the waters around Great Britain are not known as a a great cruising destination, there is limited scope for employment at sea, for example on one of the two British coastal vessels *Waverley* (a paddle steamer) and *Balmoral* of Waverley Excursions Ltd. The Scottish coastal vessel *Hebridean Princess* of Hebridean Island Cruises and Curnow Shipping's *St. Helena* (a cargo/passenger vessel that follows an interesting run from Cardiff to Cape Town and back, six times a year) also employ a certain number of people.

Everywhere Else

If you prefer to work well off the beaten seaway, why not apply to companies that specialise in expeditions, to specialist, as opposed to conventional, cruise operators, and in areas as far removed as Antarctica and Greenland? Also try freighter/cruise lines such as Ivaran Lines. Bear in mind on such trips there is no call for people to call the bingo. Entertainment programmes are replaced by lecture programmes (with great opportunities for experts in relevant fields) and excursions are planned with the adventurous in mind.

Some companies to try are:

Abercrombie & Kent–Antarctica, the Falklands, Chilean fjords, South Pacific, Amazon, etc. (with international crews)

Clipper Cruise Lines–US/Canada coastal/inland (American crews)

Hanseatic Tours–worldwide (German/European crews)

Niugini Exploration Cruises–Australia, New Guinea (local crews)

Orient Lines–see Marco Polo

Society Expeditions–worldwide (European crews)

Special Expeditions–Seychelles, Far East, Amazon, Arctic Circle, Alaska etc. (Swedish crews)

Svalbard Polar Travel–North Pole, Norway (Norwegian crews)

Temptress Cruises–Costa Rica, Belize (local crews)

World Explorer Cruises–see Universe

Charterers also sometimes have specialist staff requirements:

Classical Cruises–worldwide itineraries (international crews plus specialist lecturers in archaeology, art, etc.)

Marine Expeditions–Antarctica, Patagonia, North Cape (Russian/North American crews)

Quark Expeditions (US) and *Noble Caledonia Ltd (UK)*–marketing agents/operators for the Russian-registered ice-breakers of Murmansk Shipping and others (Antarctica, North Pole, etc.)

Southern Heritage Expeditions–Subantarctic New Zealand/Australia, Antarctic (Russian crews)

See *Cruise Ship Listing* and *Cruise Line Addresses* for further details. (Please note that not all vessels operated by the above companies are individually listed in this publication.)

Nowhere

Last but not least, we come to the 'Party Cruise' which is, in essence, the cruise to nowhere. Of course, there may be a destination, maybe even two, but the destination is not the focus. These itineraries are invariably short (usually three or four days) and are primarily aimed at that huge untapped market of people who have never before set foot on a cruise ship and are happy to spend their money. Such cruises are cheap and cheerful, in fact very cheerful, with a high rate of alcohol consumption. The passengers are much younger and noisier than the seasoned cruiser. Of course, some crew members may offer more personal services than others to ensure that their guests have a good time, while the DJ may complain at actually having to work. For stewards, barmen, croupiers and anyone else depending on tips or commission, it's one hell of a cruise. For everyone else, it's a cruise from hell.

If this sounds like your scene, try Carnival, Dolphin, Majesty, Norwegian, Premier and Royal Caribbean Cruise Line or other companies offering short cruises.

WHO OWNS THE SHIPS?

Considering that over a thousand cruise ships are currently operating around the world, including some that are more like upmarket ferries or floating casinos than cruise ships proper, keeping up with this transient industry can prove difficult.

Vessels frequently change hands and names. In recent months, several companies, including Royal Viking Line, American Family Cruises and Regency Cruises have ceased operation, while at the same time Airtours Cruises and Seawind Cruises have been formed. Cunard has been taken over by a Norwegian engineering firm; Epirotiki Lines has merged with Sun Line Cruises and formed a new parent company, Royal Olympic Cruises; Diamond Cruises and Seven Seas Cruises have merged and formed a new company called Radisson Seven Seas Cruises; and the giant Carnival Corporation (parent company of Carnival Cruise Lines) has taken over Norwegian Cruise Line (NCL), who in turn have just subsumed the Royal Cruise Line.

Some crew members may offer more personal services

Bob Williams, a seasoned ship's Hotel Manager, comments on current developments and trends in the market:

The whole business is changing and more rapidly than ever before. Certainly, there's less stability than there used to be. In fact, you can't pick up a trade magazine these days without reading that yet another company has gone bust or been taken over by someone else. Nobody in shipping presumes they're going to have a job in six months time any more.

Having said that, business is booming and cruising is still very much a growth industry. There's tremendous pressure on the companies to expand and upgrade their fleets. As I see it, it's this rapid expansion and development that is the root of the problem for some lines. They need to have new ships to keep up with their rivals, but they often can't afford what they're buying. And so, quite simply, they overspend. It's particularly hard for smaller companies to ward off the competition from 'the big boys', which is why some of them are being forced out of business or taken over.

I know that none of this is unique to cruising. Look at how small retailers are being pushed aside by the megastores. But a huge monopoly is bad for any industry and is bound to reduce the element of choice for the customer. The way things are heading, by the 21st century we'll all be cruising with one or two lines.

Taking into account the likelihood of overnight collapses, takeovers and expansions, it is advisable to consider the durability factor of companies, before applying to work for them. What follows is an alphabetical listing of the cruise companies and the ships they operate. Cruise line addresses and further information on specific vessels are given later in the book.

Bear in mind that ships are often chartered by one company from another, making it difficult to know to whom it is appropriate to apply for a job. Russian/Ukrainian companies pose particular difficulties as the same vessel may be chartered by several different (often German) operators.

While the list here does not pretend to be exhaustive, it does include the major cruise lines of interest to Western European and North American job-seekers, and the names of the ships that make up their fleets. Company names are in bold type, ships are in italics.

Abercrombie and Kent
Explorer (Expedition cruises; also markets river vessels)

Airtours Cruises
Carousel (formerly Royal Caribbeans's *Nordic Prince*)
Seawing (formerly NCL's *Southward*)
Recently-formed economy cruising division of British tour operator, and therefore a good possible starting place for would-be cruise staff.

American Hawaii Cruises
Constitution
Independence
US registry means good news for American job-seekers, but bad news for everyone else. (Very Hawaiian — bring your lei)

Arcalia Shipping
Funchal (based in Gothenburg, despite its name being the capital of Madeira; carries mostly Swedish passengers)

Ausonia Cruises
Ausonia (Italian company, possibility of jobs for linguists)

Baltic Line
Delfin Star
Ilich

Konstantin Simonov
Leonid Sobinov
These ships are often chartered by companies like CTC Cruise Lines (see below). Very Russian (good for time off in St Petersburg).

Belata Shipping Company
Maxim Gorki (frequently chartered by companies like Phoenix Reisen for mostly German passengers)

Black Sea Shipping (BLASCO)
Ayvasovsky (chartered by Eurocruises)
Azerbaydzhan (chartered by CTC for mainly British passengers)
Dimitriy Shostakovich
Fedor Dostoyevsky
Fedor Shalyapin
Ivan Franko
Kareliya (chartered by CTC for mainly British passengers)
Kazakhstan
Kazakhstan II
Lev Tolstoi (chartered by Transocean Reederei)
Odessa
Shota Rustaveli
Taras Shevchenko
These ships are generally under charter to various operators, especially German ones. See addresses in *Cruise Lines and Operators* for CTC Cruise Lines, Deutsche Seereederei, Eurocruises, Hanseatic Tours, Neckermann Seereisen, OdessAmerica Cruise Company, Phoenix Reisen and Transocean Reederei.

CTC Cruise Lines
Southern Cross (chartered from Premier for mainly British passengers)
CYC is also British agent/contact for Baltic Line, Black Sea Shipping and Far Eastern Shipping. Charterers from Black Sea Shipping.

Carnival Cruise Lines
Celebration
Destiny
Ecstasy
Fascination
Fantasy
Festivale
Holiday
Imagination
Inspiration
Jubilee
Sensation
Tropicale

Huge line with huge ships. Good for children's counsellors and party animals.

Celebrity Cruises
Century
Horizon
Meridian
Zenith
Owned by Chandris which also own Fantasy Cruises. (Don't apply to both at the same time!).

Chandris Cruises (see Celebrity and Fantasy Cruises)

Clipper Cruise Line
Nantucket Clipper
Yorktown Clipper
Great for all-American college types but, due to US registry, offer few chances to Europeans

Club Méditerranée (Club Med)
Club Med I
Club Med II
Good for water sports instructors and French-speakers.

Compagnie des Iles du Ponant
Le Ponant (good for creative chefs and French-speakers)

Costa Cruise Lines (Costa Crociere)
Costa Allegra
Costa Classica
Costa Marina
Costa Playa
Costa Riviera
Costa Romantica
Costa Victoria
Daphne
Eugenio Costa
Expanding Italian company; good for linguists and pasta lovers.

Crystal Cruises
Crystal Harmony
Crystal Symphony
5-star plus, including crew accommodation.

Cunard Line
Cunard Countess
Cunard Crown Dynasty

Royal Viking Sun
Queen Elizabeth 2
Sagafjord
Sea Goddess I
Sea Goddess II
Vistafjord
Long-established British cruise line, though with increasing American participation. Very diverse fleet.

Curnow Shipping
St Helena (cargo-passenger ship operating between Cardiff and Cape Town)

Deilmann Reederei (Peter Deilmann Shipping)
Berlin
Lili Marleen
Only worth applying if you speak German. Also operate German river boats and Sea Cloud Cruises.

Deutsche Seereederei
Aida (soon to be followed by *Aida II*)
Arkona (often chartered)
Good prospects for German-speakers (see also Black Sea Shipping)

Dolphin Cruise Line
Dolphin IV
Ocean Breeze
Sea Breeze I
Affiliated to Majesty Cruise Line. Older ships, but good for sun-seekers.

Dolphin Hellas Shipping
Aegean Dolphin (not to be confused with the previous dolphin)
Greek company. See also Viamare Travel in *Cruise Lines and Operators.*

Epirotiki Lines
Argonaut
Jason
Neptune
Odysseus
Olympic
Orpheus
Triton
World Renaissance
Mixture of European passengers and often chartered by special interest groups. Greek catering staff as well as officers but possibilities for linguists and lecturers. Recently merged with Sun Line Cruises to form Royal Olympic Cruises.

Fantasy Cruises
Amerikanis
Britanis
The 'older ship' division of Chandris Cruises.

Far Eastern Shipping Company (FESCO)
Antonina Nezhdanova
Kapitan Khlebnikov (chartered by Quark Expeditions)
Mikhail Sholokhov
Russ
See CTC Cruise Lines above. Very Russian. Some expedition cruises.

Festival Cruises
Bolero (formerly NCL's *Starward*)
The Azur
Greek line catering to Europeans. (Don't confuse Festival with Carnival)

Fred Olsen Cruises
Black Prince
Black Watch formerly the Star Odyssey of Royal Cruise Line)
Perennial British favourite. Also, British contact for Sun Line Cruises and other companies.

Hanseatic Tours
Bremen
Hanseatic
Under long-term charter from Hapag-LLoyd. Expeditions for German-speaking passengers. See also Black Sea Shipping.

Hapag-Lloyd Cruises
Europa (very German. 5-star plus for passengers and crew)
(See also the *Bremen* under Hanseatic Tours and Black Sea Shipping)

Hebridean Island Cruises
Hebridean Princess (umpteen types of whisky and an all-British crew)

Holland America Line
Maasdam
Nieuw Amsterdam
Noordam
Rotterdam
Ryndam
Statendam
Veendam
Westerdam
Major established line, now owned by Carnival, but without as many children.

Intercruise
La Palma (best prospects for Greek linguists)

Ivaran Lines
Americana (possibly the only freighter to use Gentlemen Hosts)

Kloster Cruise (see Norwegian Cruise Line)

Kristina Cruises
Kristina Regina (not worth applying to unless you're Finnish).

Louis Cruise Lines
Princesa Amorosa
Princesa Cypria
Princesa Marissa
Princesa Oceanica
Princesa Victoria
Short economy Cypriot cruises, but good for retail opportunities.

Majestic International Cruise Line
Ocean Majesty (Greek-style fun in the sun)
Chartered to major UK tour operator Page & Moy Ltd in Leicester.

Majesty Cruise Line
Royal Majesty (more Greek-style fun. Not to be confused with the Royal Princess)
Affiliated to Dolphin Cruise Line.

Mar Line
Vistamar (Hispanic passengers and Spanish officers)
See also Viamare Travel in addresses of *Cruise Lines and Operators.*

Mitsui OSK Passenger Line
Fuji Maru
Nippon Maru
Shin Sakura Maru
Of interest to Japanese-speakers only.

Murmansk Shipping
Alla Tarasova
Kapitan Dranitsyn
KlaudiaYelanskaya
Sovetskiy Soyuz
Yamal
Expeditions, and the only cruise line to hire helicopter pilots. These ships are frequently chartered by Quark Expeditions and Noble Caledonia Ltd.

Nippon Yusen Kaisha (NYK) Cruises
Asuka (5-star crew quarters for Japanese-speakers)

New Commodore Cruise Line
Enchanted Isle
Enchanted Seas
New name, same old ships. Good itineraries for sun-seekers.

Nina Cruise Line
Italia Prima (*prima* only if you speak Italian)

Noble Caledonia
Caledonian Sta (chartered to Special Expeditions)
UK agent/contact for Murmansk Shipping.

Norwegian Cruise Line (NCL)
Dreamward
Leeward
Norway
Seaward
Windward
Now owned by Carnival. Has just subsumed Royal Cruise Line (RCL) and acquired the *Crown Odyssey* (now renamed *Norwegian Crown*) and the *Royal Odyssey.*

Oceanic Cruise — see Showa Line

Orient Lines
Marco Polo (Expeditions)
British-based company, offering varied global destinations.

P & O Cruises (including P & O Holidays and P & O Spice Island Cruises)
Canberra
Fairstar (P & O Holidays, mainly Australian passengers)
Oriana
Sea Princess
Victoria
As British as Afternoon Tea, with the exception of the *Fairstar.* Part of the P & O Group which also owns Princess Cruises, Swan Hellenic Cruises and P & O European Ferries. Note that P & O Spice Island Cruises comprises several small island-hopping vessels, including the Indonesian-based Bali *Sea Dancer* (which carries mainly Greek officers and restaurant staff).

Paquet French Cruises (Croisieres Paquet)
Mermoz (good for French-speakers and classical musicians)

Paradise Cruises
Atalante
Romantica (not to be confused with the *Costa Romantica*)
Cypriot low-budget cruise line.

Premier Cruise Lines
StarShip Atlantic
StarShip Oceanic
No longer the official cruise line of Walt Disney World, but still good prospects for children's counsellors and anyone who enjoys wearing animal costumes.

Princess Cruises
Crown Princess
Golden Princess
Island Princess
Pacific Princess
Regal Princess
Royal Princess
Sky Princess
Star Princess
Sun Princess
Big American-based company, catering to big American-based passengers. Part of the P & O Group.

Radisson Seven Seas Cruises
Radisson Diamond (world's only catamaran cruise ship on which even the crew quarters are above sea level)
Song of Flower (small, deluxe, not to be confused with Royal Caribbean's *Songs*)
Result of recent merger between Diamond Cruise and Seven Seas Cruises.

Regal Cruises
Regal Empress (older ship, good for casino staff)
Confusingly, this line has nothing to do with the *Regal Princess* or Royal Cruise Line.

Renaissance Cruises
Renaissance One
Renaissance Two
Renaissance Three
Renaissance Four
Renaissance Five
Renaissance Six
Renaissance Seven
Renaissance Eight

Small ships with small crews. Frequently chartered to worldwide destinations.

Royal Caribbean Cruise Line (RCCL)
Grandeur of the Seas
Legend of the Seas
Majesty of the Seas
Monarch of the Seas
Nordic Empress
Song of America
Song of Norway
Sovereign of the Seas
Splendour of the Seas
Sun Viking (not to be confused with the *Royal Viking Sun*)
Viking Serenade
Expanding company. Good for children's staff and waiters prepared to wear fancy-dress. (Not to be confused with Royal Cruise Line/RCL.)

Royal Cruise Line (RCL)
Norwegian Crown (formerly *Crown Odyssey*)
Queen Odyssey (now sold to Seabourn)
Royal Odyssey
Now subsumed by Norwegian Cruise Line.

Royal Olympic Cruises
New parent company formed by merger of Epirotiki Lines and Sun Line Cruises. Contact via Epirotiki Lines.

Sea Cloud Cruises
Sea Cloud (magnificent sailing ship)
Operated by Deilmann Reederei. German is useful though not essential.

Seabourn Cruise Line
Seabourn Pride
Seabourn Spirit
5-star plus, including the crew accommodation

SeaEscape Cruises
Balanga Queen (Scandinavian-style, American passengers)

Seawind Cruises
Seawind Crown (Aruba-based ship not to be confused with the *Sea Wing*)

Showa Line (including Oceanic Cruise)
Oceanic Grace (good for watersports instructors, since it is the only cruise ship with a scuba decompression chamber).
Very Japanese. Chefs/hotel staff provided by Tokyo's Palace Hotel.

Siam Cruise Company
Andaman Princess (only if you speak Thai)

Silversea Cruises
Silver Cloud
Silver Wind
Operated by V-ships, good for watersports instructors, since it carries kayaks.

Society Expeditions
World Discoverer (worldwide expeditions)

Special Expeditions
Polaris (worldwide soft expeditions).
Mainly British passengers. Also charterers from Noble Caledonia.

Star Cruise
MegaStar Aries
MegaStar Taurus
Star Aquarius
Star Pisces
SuperStar Gemini (formerly *Crown Jewel*)
Expanding company offering eastern promise to Asian language-speakers.

Star Clippers Inc
Star Clipper
Star Flyer
Luxury sail-cruise ships. Perfect for water sports instructors and proper sailors.

StarLauro Cruises
Monterey
Rhapsody (until recently, the *Cunard Princess* bought to replace the sunken *Achille Lauro*)
Symphony (formerly the *Enrico Costa)*
These ships offer a mixture of British and Italian passengers, with an Italian-speaking staff.

Starline Cruises
Royal Star (operated by the African Safari Club hotel group, not to be confused with any other 'stars' or 'royals')

Sun Line Cruises
Stella Maris
Stella Oceanis
Stella Solaris

Recently merged with Epirotiki Lines to form Royal Olympic Cruises, with predominantly Greek staff. See also Fred Olsen Cruises.

Swan Hellenic Cruises
Minerva (varied itineraries for mainly British passengers)
Part of the P & O Group. Swan Hellenic also markets river cruises.

Tall Ship Adventures
Sir Francis Drake (sailing ship for adventurous rig-scalers)

V-Ships
Albatros (chartered to Phoenix Reisen for German passengers)
Operator for Silversea Cruises and also a catering concessionaire.

Windstar Cruises
Wind Song (based in French Polynesia)
Wind Spirit
Wind Star
Good for watersports instructors and British officers.

World Explorer Cruises
Universe (Alaska-based cargo-cruise ship with Chinese officers and Gentlemen Hosts)

CRUISE LINE ADDRESSES

Please note that the following list of addresses and (especially) telephone numbers is subject to change. Details should always be verified before posting applications, expensive publicity packages, etc. Never send originals of references or photographs and other material that you do not intend the receiver to keep. Even stamped addressed envelopes and offers of return postage will not always get them back.

If telephoning, be advised that the code for the US from Great Britain is 001; the code for the UK from the Unites States is 00144. For all other countries, dial 00+ the country code (given in brackets before the number).

Note: An asterisk (*) is not intended as a recommendation, only as a sign that the company in question may be able to offer a wider choice of general job opportunities because of the size of their fleets and their passenger/crew nationality breakdowns (details in *Cruise Ship Listing* above).

Abercrombie & Kent,
Sloane Square House, Holbein Place, London SW1W 8NS
Tel: 0171-730 9600
Also:

1520 Kensington Rd, Oak Brook, IL 60521, USA
Tel: 708-954-2944

Airtours Cruises,
Overseas Recruitment, Wavell House, Holcombe Rd, Helmshore, Ros-
sendale, Lancs. BB4 4NB
Tel: 01706 240033

Alaska Sightseeing/Cruise West (Coastal),
4th and Battery Building, Suite 700, Seattle, WA 98121, USA
Tel: 206-441-8687

Amazon Tours and Cruises,
8700 West Flagler St, Miami, FL 33174, USA
Tel: 305-227-2266

American Canadian Caribbean Line (rivers/coastal),
461 Water St, PO Box 368, Warren, RI 02885, USA
Tel: 401-247-0955

American Hawaii Cruises,
550 Kearney St, San Francisco, CA 94108, USA
Tel: 312-466-6000

American West Steamship Company (river cruises),
520 Pike St, Suite 1400, Seattle, WA 98101, USA
Tel: 206-292-9606

Arcalia Shipping,
Av 24 de Julho, 126/128–53, 1300 Lisbon, Portugal
Tel: (351) 1-395-3233

Ausonia Cruises,
Via C. D'Andrea, 80133 Naples, Italy
Tel: (39) 81-551-7755

Baltic Line,
Mezhevoy Kanal 5, 198035 St Petersburg, Russia
Tel: (7) 812-1149720
(See also CTC Cruise Lines)

Belata Shipping Company,
c/o Unicorn Management Services Ltd, 2nd Floor, Oasis Center, PO
Box 6674, Limassol, Cyprus
Tel: (357) 05-343131

Black Sea Shipping (BLASCO),

ul. Lastochkina 1, 270026 Odessa, Ukraine
Tel: (380) 48-7095-252160 or 224893
(See also CTC Cruise Lines)

CTC Cruise Lines,
1 Regent St, London SW1Y 4NN
Tel: 0171-896 8844
(British agent/contact for Black Sea Shipping, Baltic Line and Far Eastern Shipping Company)

*Carnival Cruise Lines,
3655 NW 87th Avenue, Miami, FL 33178, USA
Tel: 305-599-2600
Also:
Walter House, 418-422 Strand, London WC2R 0PT
Tel: 0171-240 8471

Celebrity Cruises,
See Chandris Cruises

*Chandris Cruises (incorporating Celebrity and Fantasy Cruises),
5200 Blue Lagoon Drive, Miami, FL 33126, USA
Tel: 305-262-6677
Also:
17 Old Park Lane, London W1Y 3LH
Tel: 0171-412 3999

China Yangtze River Shipping Company,
89 Yanjiang Dadao, Hankou, Wuhan, Hubei Province 430000, China
Tel: (86) 27-281-4543

Classical Cruises (specialist charterer),
132 East 70th St, New York, NY 10021, USA
Tel: 212-794-3200

Clipper Cruise Line,
7711 Bonhomme Avenue, St Louis, MO 63105, USA
Tel: 314-727-2929

Club Mediterranée (Club Med),
40 West 57 St, New York, NY 10019, USA
Tel: 212-977-2100
Also:
106-110 Brompton Rd, London SW3 1JJ
Tel: 0171-225 1066

Compagnie des Iles du Ponant,
60 Boulevard Marechal Juin, 44100 Nantes, France

Tel: (33) 1-40 58 14 95

*Costa Cruise Lines (Costa Crociere),
World Trade Center, 80 SW 8th St, Miami, FL 33130-3097, USA
Tel: 305-358-7325
Also:
Albany House, 45-49 Mortimer St, London W1N 8JL
Tel: 0171-223 2200
Also:
VC 11 San Nicola Alla Dogana 9/32, Napoli, Italy
Tel: (39) 81-551-2483

Crystal Cruises,
2121 Avenue of the Stars, Los Angeles, CA 90067, USA
Tel: 310-785-9300
(See also Paul Mundy Ltd)

*Cunard Line,
South Western House, Canute Rd, Southampton SO9 1ZA
Tel: 01703 716500
Also:
555 Fifth Avenue, New York, NY 10017, USA
Tel: 212-880-7500

Cunard EuropAmerica River Cruises
See Cunard Line and Deilmann Reederei

Curnow Shipping,
The Shipyard, Porthleven, Helston, Cornwall TR13 9JA
Tel: 01326-563434

Deilmann Reederei (Peter Deilmann Shipping),
Am Hafensteig 19, D-2430 Neustadt in Holstein, Germany
Tel: (49) 4561-61060
(Operator of Sea Cloud Cruises and river cruises; marketed by Cunard
EuropAmerica River Cruises)

Delta Queen Steamboat Company,
30 Robin Street Wharf, New Orleans, LA 70130, USA
Tel: 504-586-0631

Deutsche Seereederei,
PO Box 102188, 18003 Rostock, Germany
Tel: (49) 0381-458-4097

Dirigo Cruises (sailing ships),
39 Waterside Lane, Clinton, CT 06413, USA
Tel: 203-669-7068

Disney Cruise Lines,
210 Celebration Place, Suite 400, Celebration, FL 34747-4600, USA
Tel: 407-934-7639
(First ship to be launched in 1998)

Dolphin Cruise Line,
901 South America Way, Miami, FL 33132-2073, USA
Tel: 305-358-2111

Dolphin Hellas Shipping,
71 Miaouli Akti, 185 37 Piraeus, Greece
Tel: (30) 1-45-12109
(See also Viamare Travel Ltd)

*Epirotiki Lines,
87 Miaouli Akti, 185 38 Piraeus, Greece
Tel: (30) 1-42-91000
Also:
551 Fifth Avenue, New York, NY 10176, USA
Tel: 212-949-7273
Also:
Westmorland House, 127 Regent St, London W1R 7HA
Tel: 0171-734 1487
(See also Royal Olympic Cruises)

Equity Cruises,
77-79 Great Eastern St, London EC2A 3HU
Tel: 0171-729 1929
(British agent/contact for Intercruise, Starlauro, etc.)

Eurocruises (rivers/coastal),
303 West 13th St, New York, NY 10014, USA
Tel: 212-691-2099

Fantasy Cruises,
See Chandris Cruises

Far Eastern Shipping Company (FESCO),
ul. Aleutskaya 15, 690019 Vladivostok, Russia
Tel: (7) 4232-222432 or 225391
(See also CTC Cruise Lines)

Festival Cruises,
99 Miaouli Akti, GR 185 38, Piraeus, Greece
Tel: (30) 1-42-90769
Also:
404 Albany House, 324 Regent St, London W1R, 5AA
Tel: 0171-436 6684

Fred Olsen Cruises,
Fred Olsen House, Whitehouse Rd, Ipswich, Suffolk 1P1 5LL
Tel: 01473 233066
(Also British agent/contact for Sun Line Cruises etc.)

Hanseatic Tours,
Nagelsweg 55, D-20097 Hamburg, Germany
Tel: (49) 40-239-1103

Hapag-Lloyd Cruises,
PO Box 102626, Hapag Lloyd Haus, Ballindamm 25, DW-2000 Hamburg 1, Germany
Tel: (49) 40-30010

Hebridean Island Cruises,
Acorn Park, Skipton, N. Yorkshire BD23 2UE
Tel: 01756 701380

Hilton Nile Cruises (river cruises),
c/o Nile Hilton, PO Box 257, Cairo, Egypt
Tel: (202) 5780-444
(See also Misr Travel)

*Holland America Line,
300 Elliott Avenue West, Seattle, WA 98119, USA
Tel: 206-281-3535

Intercruise,
126 Kolokotroni St, 185 35 Piraeus, Greece
Tel: (30) 1-42-83484
(See also Equity Cruises)

Ivaran Lines,
Newport Financial Center, 111 Pavonia Ave, Jersey City, NY 07310-1755, USA
Tel: 201-798-5656

KD German Rhine Line,
15 Frankenwert, 50667 Köln, Germany
Tel: (49) 221-20880
Also:
28 South St, Epsom, Surrey KT18 7PF
Tel: 01372 742033

Kloster Cruise (used to incorporate Royal Cruise Line/RCL: now subsumed by Norwegian Cruise Line),
95 Merrick Way, Coral Gables, FL 33134, USA
Tel: 305-447-9660

Also:
Brook House, 229 Shepherds Bush Rd, Hammersmith, London W6 7NL
Tel: 0171-493 6041

Kristina Cruises,
Rannikolininjat OY, Korkeavouenkatu 2, SF-48100 Helsinki, Finland
Tel: (358) 0-629968

Louis Cruise Lines,
158 Franklin Roosevelt and Omonia Avenues, Limassol, Cyprus
Tel: (357) 5-374063

Maine Windjammers (sailing ships),
Box 482, Rockland, ME 04841, USA
Tel: 207-594-8007

Majestic International Cruise Line,
See Page & Moy Ltd

Majesty Cruise Line,
901 South America Way, Miami FL 33132-2073, USA
Tel: 305-530-8900

Mar Line,
Akti Possidonos 38, 18531 Piraeus, Greece
Tel: (30) 1-42-24-950
(See also Viamare Travel)

Marine Expeditions (charterer),
13 Hazelton Avenue, Toronto, Ontario M5R 2E1, Canada
Tel: (001) 416-964-9069

Misr Travel,
201-204 2nd Floor, 308 Langham House, Regent St, London W1R 5AL
Tel: 0171-255 1087
(Operator for Nile cruises, incorporating Sheraton and Hilton Nile
Cruises)

Mitsui OSK Passenger Line,
Shosen Mitsui Bldg, 1 Toranomon, 2-Chrome, Minato-Ku, Tokyo 105,
Japan
Tel: (81) 3-358-77111

Moorings (see The Moorings)

Murmansk Shipping,
ul. Kominterna 15, 183636 Murmansk, Russia

Tel: (7) 8152-522451 or 522201
(See also Quark Expeditions and Noble Caledonia)

NYK (Nippon Yusen Kaisha) Cruises,
3-2 Marunouchi 2-Chome, Chiyoda-Ku, Tokyo 100, Japan
Tel: (81) 3-328-45151

Nautical Resources, Inc (yacht crews),
666 Fifth Avenue, New York, NY 10103, USA
Tel: 800-398-6244

Neckermann Seereisen (charterer),
Zimmersmuehlenweg 55, 61440 Oberursel, Germany
Tel: (49) 6172-92520

New Commodore Cruise Line,
4000 Hollywood Boulevard, 385 South Tower, Hollywood, FL 33021,
USA
Tel: 305-967-2105

Nina Cruise Line,
404 Albany House, 324-326 Regent St, London W1R 5AA
Tel: 0171-436-6684
Also:
Via T Galimberti 7/2, 16128 Genoa, Italy
Tel: (39) 10-588911

Niugini Exploration Cruises,
302 West Grand Avenue, Suite 10B, El Segundo, CA 90245, USA
Tel: 213-785-0370

Noble Caledonia,
11 Charles St, Mayfair London W1X 8LE
Tel: 0171-355 1424
(British operator/contact for Murmansk Shipping, etc.)

*Norwegian Cruise Line (NCL),
95 Merrick Way, Coral Gables, FL 33134, USA
Tel: 305-447-9660
Also:
Brook House, 229 Shepherds Bush Rd, Hammersmith, London W6 7NL
Tel: 0171-493 6041

Oberoi Nile Cruises,
1 Thames Place, Lower Richmond Rd, London SW15 1HF
Tel: 0181-788 2070

Oceanic Cruise,

See Showa Line Ltd

OdessAmerica Cruise Company (charterer),
170 Old Country Rd, Mineola, NY 11501, USA
Tel: 800-221-3254

Orient Express Cruises (river cruises),
c/o Orient Express Hotels, 1155 Avenue of the Americas, New York,
NY, USA
Tel: 212-302-5055

Orient Lines,
38 Park St, London W1Y 3PF
Tel: 0171-409 7500

*P & O Cruises,
Richmond House, Terminus Terrace, Southampton SO14 3PN
Tel: 01703 534200

P & O Holidays/P & O Spice Island Cruises
See P & O Cruises

Page & Moy Ltd
c/o Cruise Product Manager, 136-140 London Rd, Leicester LE2 1EN
Tel: 0116-252 6121
(Cruising specialist and charterer/contact for Majestic International
Cruise Line)

Paquet French Cruises (Croisieres Paquet),
5 Boulevard Malesherbes, F-75008, Paris, France
Tel: (33) 1-49 24 94 20

Paradise Cruises,
52 Kitiou Kyprianou St, PO Box 157, Limassol, Cyprus
Tel: (357) 5-357604

Paul Mundy,
11 Quadrant Arcade, Regent St, London W1R 6JB
Tel: 0171-734 4404
(British agent/contact for Crystal Cruises, etc.)

Phoenix Reisen (charterer),
Koelnstrasse 80, 53111 Bonn, Germany
Tel: (49) 228-726-2859

Premier Cruise Lines,
400 Challenger Rd, Cape Canaveral, FL 32920, USA
Tel: 407-783-5061

Also:
90 High Rd, Broxbourne, Herts. EN10 7DZ
Tel: 01992 441517

*Princess Cruises,
77 New Oxford St, London WC1A 1PP
Tel: 0171-800 2345
Also:
10100 Santa Monica Blvd, Los Angeles, CA 90067, USA
Tel: 310-553-1770

Quark Expeditions,
980 Post Rd, Darien, CT 06820, USA
Tel: 203-656-0499
(American operator/contact for Murmansk Shipping)

Radisson Seven Seas Cruises,
600 Corporate Drive, Suite 410, Fort Lauderdale, FL 33334, USA
Tel: 800-477-7500
Also:
38 St Martins Lane, London WC2N 4ER
Tel: 0171-240 0576

Regal China Cruises (riverboats),
57 W. 38th St, New York, NY, USA
Tel: 212-768-3388
(See Abercrombie & Kent)

Regal Cruises,
c/o International Shipping Partners Inc, Suite 30A, Penthouse A, 555
NE 15th St, Miami, FL 33132, USA
Tel: 305-573-6355

Renaissance Cruises,
1800 Eller Drive, Suite 300, PO Box 350307, Fort Lauderdale, FL
33335-0307, USA
Tel: 305-463-0982

*Royal Caribbean Cruise Line,
1050 Caribbean Way, Miami, FL 33132-2601, USA
Tel: 305-539-6000
Also:
Royal Caribbean House, Addlestone Rd, Weybridge, Surrey KT15 2UE
Tel: 01932 820230

*Royal Cruise Line
One Maritime Plaza, Suite 660, San Francisco, CA 94111, USA
Tel: 415-956-7200
Also:

81 Akti Miaouli, 185-38 Piraeus, Greece
Tel: (30) 1-428-0015
(Now subsumed by Norwegian Cruise Line)

Royal Olympic Cruises
New parent company of Epirotiki Lines and Sun Line Cruises. Contact via Epirotiki Lines

St Lawrence Cruise Lines (riverboats),
253 Ontario St, Kingston, Ontario K7L 2Z4, Canada
Tel: (001) 613-549-8091

Sacks Yacht Charters,
1600 Southeast 17th St, Suite 418, Fort Lauderdale, FL 33316, USA
Tel: 305-764-7742

Sea Cloud Cruises,
See Deilmann Reederei

Seabourn Cruise Line,
55 Francisco St, Suite 210, San Francisco, CA 94133, USA
Tel: 415-391-7444
Also:
Norway House, 21-24 Cockspur St, London W1Y 5BN
Tel: 0171-930 4447

SeaEscape Cruises,
1080 Port Blvd, Miami, FL33132
Tel: 305-377-9000

Seawind Cruises,
Bay Point Office Tower, 4770 Biscayne Boulevard, Suite 1470, Miami, Florida, USA
Tel: 305-573-5640

Seetours International (charterer),
Seilerstrasse 23, 60313 Frankfurt, Germany
Tel: (49) 691-3330

Sheraton Nile Cruises (river cruises),
Ahmed Pacha St 4, Garden City, Cairo, Egypt
Tel: (20) 2-355-6664
(See also Misr Travel)

Showa Line (incorporating Oceanic Cruise),
Hibiya Kokusai Building, 2-3 Uchisaiwai -cho 2-chome, Chiyoda-ku, Tokyo 100, Japan

Tel: (81) 3-3581-8631

Siam Cruise Company,
Chaiyod Arcade, 33/10-11, Sukhumvit Soi 11 Rd, Klongtoey, Phrak-anong, Bangkok 10110, Thailand
Tel: (66) 2-255-8950

Silversea Cruises,
110 Broward Blvd, Fort Lauderdale, FL 33301, USA
Tel: 305-522-4477

Society Expeditions,
2001 Western Avenue, Suite 300, Seattle, WA 98121, USA
Tel: 800-548-8669

Sonnesta Hotels (Nile Cruises),
4 El Tayaran St, Nasr City, Cairo, Egypt
Tel: (20) 2-262-8111

Southern Heritage Expeditions (charterer),
6033 West Century Boulevard, No. 1270, Los Angeles, CA 90045, USA
Tel: 310-338-1538

Special Expeditions,
720 Fifth Ave, Suite 605, New York, NY 10019, USA
Tel: 212-765-7740

Star Cruise,
391B Orchard Rd, 13-01 Ngee Ann City Tower B, Singapore 0923
Tel: (65) 733-6388

Star Clippers Inc
4101 Salzedo St, Coral Gables, FL 33146, USA
Tel: 305-442-0550

Starlauro Cruises,
Piazza Garibaldi 91, 80142 Napoli, Italy
Tel: (39) 81-554-54-11
(See also Equity Cruises)

Starline Cruises,
1 Duckett's Wharf, 109 South St, Bishop's Stortford, Herts. CM23 3AR
Tel: 01279 465846

Sun Line Cruises,
One Rockefeller Plaza, Suite 315, New York, NY 10020, USA
Tel: 212-397-6400

(See also Royal Olympic Cruises and Fred Olsen Cruises)

Svalbard Polar Travel (expeditions),
303 West 13th St, New York, NY 10014, USA
Tel: 212-691-2099

Swan Hellenic Cruises (subsidiary of the P & O Group),
77 New Oxford St, London WC1A 1DS
Tel: 0171-800 2200
Also:
581 Boylston St, Boston, MA 02116, USA
Tel: 617-266-7465

Tall Ship Adventures,
1010 Joliet St, Suite 200, Aurora, CO 80012, USA
Tel: 303-342-0335

Temptress Cruises (Costa Rican expeditions),
1600 Northwest LeJeune Rd, Suite 301, Miami, FL 33126, USA
Tel: 305-871-2663

The Moorings (yacht crews),
19345 US Highway 19 North, 4th Floor, Clearwater, FL 34624, USA
Tel: 813-535-1446

Transocean Reederei,
Palmaille 45, Postfach 501522, 22767 Hamburg, Germany
Tel: (49) 40-380160
(Agent/charterer of Black Sea Shipping)

V-Ships,
Aigue Marine, 24 Avenue de Fontvieille, PO Box 639, MC 98013, Monaco
Tel: (3393) 9205-1010

Viamare Travel,
Graphic House, 2 Sumatra Rd, London NW6 1PV
Tel: 0171-431 4560
(British agent/contact for Dolphin Hellas and Mar Line)

Victoria Cruises (Yangtze river cruises),
57-08 39th Avenue Woodside, New York, NY 11377, USA
Tel: 212-818-1680

Waverley Excursions Ltd (British Coastal),
Anderston Quay, Glasgow G3 8HA, Scotland
Tel: 0141-221-8152

Windjammer Barefoot Cruises (sailing ships),
Box 120, Miami Beach, FL 33139, USA
Tel: 305-672-6453

Windstar Cruises,
300 Elliott Avenue West, Seattle, WA 98119, USA
Tel: 206-281-3535
Also:
PO Box, Standard House, 15-16 Bonhill St, London EC2P 2EA
Tel: 0171-628-7711

World Explorer Cruises,
555 Montgomery Ave, San Francisco, CA 94111, USA
Tel: 415-391-9262

Worldwide Travel & Cruise Associates (sailing ships),
400 SE 12th St, Fort Lauderdale, FL 33316, USA
Tel: 305-463-1922

Zeus Cruises (sailing yachts),
566 Seventh Avenue, New York, NY 10018, USA
Tel: 212-221-0006.

CARGO AND FERRY COMPANIES

Alaska State Ferries,
Homer Ferry Terminal, PO Box 166, Homer, AK 99603, USA
Tel: 800-382-9229

Bergen Line (Norwegian coastal),
405 Park Avenue, New York, NY 10022, USA
Tel: 212-319-1300

British Columbia Ferries,
1112 Fort St, Victoria, British Columbia V8V 4V2, Canada
Tel: (Canada-001) 604-386-3431

Brittany Ferries,
Gare Maritime, Port du Bloscon (Boite Postale 72), 29211 Roscoff,
France
Tel: (33) 98 29 28 00
Also:
The Brittany Centre, Wharf Road, Portsmouth PO2 8RU
Tel: 01705 751708

Brittany Channel Island Ferries,
(See Truckline Ferries)

Caledonian MacBrayne,
Ferry Terminal, Ardrossan, Ayrshire KA22 8EW, Scotland
Tel: 01294 63470

Color Line,
Tyne Commission Quay, North Shields, Tyne & Wear, NE29 6EA
Tel: 0191-296 1313

DFDS,
Sankt Anna Plads 30, DK-1295 Copenhagen K, Denmark
Tel: (45) 33 42 33 42

Hapag-Lloyd Ferries,
Ballindamm 25, Postach 102 626, Hamburg, Germany
Tel: (49) 403 00 10
Staff must be German-speaking

Irish Ferries,
Dublin Ferryport, Alexandra Road, Dublin 1, Co. Dublin, Eire
Tel: (353) 1-855 2222
Also:
3rd Floor, 35 Dover St, London W1X 3RA
Tel: 0171-499 5744

Minoan Lines Shipping,
4 Astigos St, 18531 Piraeus, Greece
Tel: (30) 1-413 6103
Also:
38 Agiou Titou St, PO Box 1120, 71202 Iraklion, Crete, Greece
Tel: (30) 81-229202

North Sea Ferries,
King George Dock, Hedon Road, Hull HU9 5QA
Tel: 01482 795141

P & O European Ferries,
Richmond House, Terminus Terrace, Southampton, Hants. SO14 3PN
Tel: 01703 534200
Also:
Peninsular House, Wharf Road, Portsmouth PO2 8TA
Tel: 01705 772000

Sally Line,
Argyle Centre, York St, Ramsgate, Kent, CT11 9DS
Tel: 01843 595566

Scandinavian Seaways,
Scandinavian House, Parkstone Quay, Harwich, Essex CO12 4QG
Tel: 01255 240240

Stena Line,
Charter House, Park St, Ashford, Kent TN24 8EX
Tel: 01233 647022
Also:
The Stena Group,
PO Box 31300, S-40519 Gothenburg, Sweden
Tel: (46) 31 85 80 00

Truckline Ferries,
New Harbour Road, Poole BH15 4AJ
Tel: 01202 441120
(Also, administrative centre for Brittany Channel Island Ferries)

OTHER USEFUL ADDRESSES

British & International Sailors' Society,
Seafarers' Centre, 2-3 Orchard Place, Southampton, Hants. SO14 3AT
Tel: 01703 337333
Also:
Seafarers' Helpline in UK: 0800-220393

CLIA (Cruise Lines International Association)
500 Fifth Avenue, Suite 1407, New York, NY 10110, USA
Tel: 212-921-0066

The Marine Society,
202 Lambeth Road, London SE1 7JW
Tel: 0171-261 9535

NUMAST (National Union of Marine, Aviation and Shipping Transport Officers),
Oceanair House, 750-760 High Road, Leytonstone, London E11 3BB
Tel: 0181-989 6677

National Union of Rail, Maritime and Transport Workers,
Unity House, 205 Euston Road, London NW1 2BL
Tel: 0171-387 4771

PSARA (Passenger Shipping Association of Retail Agents),
9-10 Market Place, London W1N 7AG
Tel: 0171-436 2449

CRUISE SHIP LISTING

The following pages provide valuable information for potential crew members. For each ship listed it is possible to ascertain:

a) name of operating company or shipping line
b) area/s of the world in which the ship cruises
c) length of average cruise
d) nationality of most officers
e) nationality of majority of dining room staff
f) maximum passenger carry
g) total number of crew members

By referring to this list, you will be able to decide which companies and vessels are most likely to suit your preferences and requirements. Please note that all figures given are approximate and for guidance only. Inevitable changes in the cruising industry may render some entries obsolete within the lifetime of this book.

Abbreviations

Afr = Africa(n)	Exp = Expeditions	Med = Mediterranean
Am = American	Fil = Filipino	Nor = Norwegian
Ant = The Antarctic	Fr = French	Oc = Ocean
Arc = The Arctic	Ger = German	Rus = Russian
Bri = British	Gr = Greek	Sca = Scandinavian
Can = Canada/ian	Ind = Indonesian	Spa = Spanish
Carib = Caribbean	Int = International	UK = United Kingdom
Ch = Chinese	It = Italian	Ukr = Ukrainian
Dut = Dutch	Jap = Japanese	US = United States
Eur = Europe/European		

In addition, compass points (N, S, E, W) may prefix regions and a plus sign (+) means 'and upwards', e.g. 7+ means that cruises last at least seven nights.

For ease of reference, the list is coded in this way:

Name of ship - (a) Name of operating company

(b) Area in which the ship is based (c) Number of nights of average cruise	(d) Nationality of the officers	(e) Nationality of the dining room staff	(f) Maximum number of passengers	(g) Usual number of crew

Example:

Windward - Norwegian Cruise Line

Alaska/Carib (7)	Nor	Int	1450	480

From this example, one can ascertain that the cruise liner Windward is operated by Norwegian Cruise Line. It spends part of the year in Alaska and part in the

Caribbean, each cruise usually lasting seven days. Her officers are mainly Norwegian, although the dining room staff is international. She carries a maximum of 1,450 passengers (bear in mind that few cruises are ever full to capacity) and an approximate total of 480 crew members.

Aegean Dolphin - Dolphin Hellas Shipping
Med (3-7)   Gr   Int   600   200

Aida - Deutsche Seereederei
World (various)   Ger   Ger   1150   370

Albatros - V-Ships
Eur (7)   It   Int   1000   300

Alla Tarasova - Murmansk Shipping
Ant/Arc (Exp)   Rus   E.Eur   100   80

Americana - Ivaran Lines
S.America (51)   Nor   S.Am   100   45

Amerikanis - Fantasy Cruises
Eur (7)   Gr   Int   600   400

Andaman Princess - Siam Cruise Company
Thailand (7)   Thai   Thai   350   200

Antonina Nezhdanova - Far Eastern Shipping Company
Various   Rus   Rus   180   100

Argonaut - Epirotiki Lines
Eur (various)   Gr   Gr   180   100

Arkona - Deutsche Seereederei
Eur (various)   Ger   Eur   500   240

Asuka - NYK Cruises
Asia (various)   Jap   Mixed   600   240

Atalante - Paradise Cruises
Med (3/4)   Gr   Int   630   160

Ausonia - Ausonia Cruises
Eur (6-11)   It   It   800   200

Ayvasovsky - Black Sea Shipping (see Eurocruises)
Black Sea/Med (7)   Ukr   Ukr   250   130

Azerbaydzhan - Black Sea Shipping (see CTC Cruise Lines)
Various   Ukr   Eur   630   240

Balanga Queen - SeaEscape Cruises
Carib (various)   Nor   Int   1,100   500

Berlin - Deilmann Reederei
World (various)	Ger	Ger	440	200

Black Prince - Fred Olsen Cruises
Eur (14)	Eur	Fil	500	200

Bolero - Festival Cruises
Med (7)	Nor	Int	750	310

Bremen - Hapag-Lloyd Cruises (see Hanseatic Tours)
World (Exp)	Eur	Fil	180	90

Britanis - Fantasy Cruises
Carib (7)	Gr	Int	900	520

Caledonian Star - Noble Caledonia (see Special Expeditions)
World (Exp)	Sca	Int	170	60

Canberra - P & O Cruises
Eur (14)	Bri	Bri	1600	850

Carousel - Airtours Cruises
Med (7)	Eur	Int	1000	430

Celebration - Carnival Cruise Lines
Carib (7)	It	Int	1800	650

Century - Celebrity Cruises
Carib (various)	Gr	Int	1750	850

Club Med I - Club Mediterranée
Carib/Eur (7)	Fr	Int	400	180

Club Med II - Club Mediterranée
S.Pacific (various)	Fr	Int	400	180

Constitution - American Hawaii Cruises
Hawaii (7)	Am	Am	1000	300

Costa Allegra - Costa Cruise Lines (Costa Crociere)
Med/Carib (7-13)	It	Int	1000	400

Costa Classica - Costa Cruise Lines (Costa Crociere)
Med/Carib (7)	It	Int	1750	600

Costa Marina - Costa Cruise Lines (Costa Crociere)
Med/S.Am (6-14)	It	Int	1000	400

Costa Playa - Costa Cruise Lines (Costa Crociere)
Carib (7)	Bri	Int	480	230

Costa Riviera - Costa Cruise Lines (Costa Crociere)
Carib/Med (7)	It	Int	900	650

Costa Romantica - Costa Cruise Lines (Costa Crociere)
| Carib/Med (7) | It | Int | 1750 | 600 |

Costa Victoria - Costa Cruise Lines (Costa Crociere)
| Carib (various) | It | Int | 1950 | 750 |

Crown Odyssey - Royal Cruise Line
| World (various) | Gr | Gr | 1200 | 470 |

Crown Princess - Princess Cruises
| Alask/Carib (7) | It | Int | 1900 | 700 |

Crystal Harmony - Crystal Cruises
| World (various) | Sca/Jap | Eur/Fil | 950 | 540 |

Crystal Symphony - Crystal Cruises
| Various | Sca | Eur | 950 | 540 |

Cunard Countess - Cunard Line
| Carib (7-14) | Bri | Int | 900 | 360 |

Cunard Crown Dynasty - Cunard Line
| Alaska/Carib (7) | Bri | Eur | 900 | 330 |

Daphne - Costa Cruise Lines (Costa Crociere)
| Med (12) | It | Int | 500 | 260 |

Delfin Star - Baltic Line
| Baltic (3/4) | Sca | Sca | 300 | 70 |

Destiny - Carnival Cruise Lines
| Carib (7) | It | Int | 2650 | 1000 |

Dimitriy Shostakovich - Black Sea Shipping
| Eur (14) | Rus/Uk | E.Eur | 490 | 150 |

Dolphin IV - Dolphin Cruise Line
| Bahamas (2) | Gr | Int | 680 | 300 |

Dreamward - Norwegian Cruise Line
| Bermuda/Carib (7) | Nor | Int | 1450 | 480 |

Ecstasy - Carnival Cruise Lines
| Carib (3/4) | It | Int | 2550 | 900 |

Enchanted Isle - New Commodore Cruise Line
| Mexico (7) | Eur | Int | 720 | 350 |

Enchanted Seas - New Commodore Cruise Line
| Carib (7) | Eur | Int | 740 | 360 |

Enrico Costa - Costa Cruise Lines (Costa Crociere)
Med (6-11)   It   Int   840   330

Eugenio Costa - Costa Cruise Lines (Costa Crociere)
Med/S.Am (4-14)   It   Int   1400   480

Europa - Hapag-Lloyd Cruises
World (various)   Ger   Eur   600   300

Explorer - Abercrombie & Kent
World (Exp)   Eur   Eur/Fil   100   70

Fairstar - P & O Holidays (P & O Cruises)
Asia/S.Pac (14)   It   It/Ind   1500   460

Fantasy - Carnival Cruise Lines
Bahamas (3/4)   It   Int   2600   900

Fascination - Carnival Cruise Lines
Carib (7)   It   Int   2500   900

Fedor Dostoyevsky - Black Sea Shipping
World (various)   Rus   E.Eur   650   300

Fedor Shalyapin - Black Sea Shipping
Eur (various)   Rus   E.Eur   800   380

Festivale - Carnival Cruise Lines
Carib (7)   It   Int   1400   580

Fuji Maru - Mitsui OSK Line
Asia (various)   Jap   Jap/Fil   600   200

Funchal - Arcalia Shipping
Eur (various)   Eur   Eur   460   150

Golden Princess - Princess Cruises
Alaska/Mex (7-10)   Sca   Int   860   430

Grandeur of the Seas - Royal Caribbean Cruise Line
Carib (various)   Nor   Int   1950   760

Hanseatic - Hanseatic Tours
World (Exp)   Ger   Int   200   120

Hebridean Princess - Hebridean Island Cruises
Scotland (7)   Bri   Bri   55   35

Holiday - Carnival Cruise Lines
Carib (7)   It   Int   1800   660

Horizon - Celebrity Cruises
Alaska/Carib (7)   Gr   Int   1650   640

Holiday - Carnival Cruise Lines

Carib (7)	It	Int	2500	900

Ilich - Baltic Line

Baltic (2-5)	Rus	Ukr/Sca	380	160

Imagination - Carnival Cruise Lines

W.Carib (7)	It	Int	2000	900

Independence - American Hawaii Cruises

Hawaii (7)	Am	Am	1000	300

Inspiration - Carnival Cruise Lines

Carib (7)	It	Int	2000	900

Island Princess - Princess Cruises

Various	Bri	Int	700	350

Italia Prima - Nina Cruise Line

World (various)	It	It	600	260

Ivan Franko - Black Sea Shipping

Eur (various)	Rus	Ukr	700	340

Jason - Epirotiki Lines

Eur (3-7)	Gr	Gr	300	140

Jubilee - Carnival Cruise Lines

Mexico (7)	It	Int	1800	670

Kapitan Dranitsyn - Murmansk Shipping (Quark Exp.)

Ant/Arc (Exp)	Rus	Rus/Ukr	110	90

Kapitan Khlebnikov - Far Eastern Shipping Co. (Quark Exp.)

Ant/Polar (Exp)	Rus	Rus/Ukr	110	90

Kareliya - Black Sea Shipping (see CTC Cruise Lines)

Eur (7)	Ukr	Bri/Ukr	640	250

Kazakhstan - Black Sea Shipping

Eur (various)	Rus/Ukr	Rus/Ukr	640	250

Kazakhstan II - Black Sea Shipping

World (various)	Ukr	Ukr	640	250

Klaudia Yelanskaya - Murmansk Shipping

Arctic (Exp)	Rus	Rus/Ukr	180	80

Konstantin Simonov - Baltic Line

Baltic (3)	Rus	Rus	490	160

Kristina Regina - Kristina Cruises
Baltic (10-14)   Fin   Fin   350   55

La Palma - Intercruise
Eur (7-11)   Gr   830   230   230

Le Ponant - Compagnie des Iles du Ponant
Carib (7)   Fr   Fr   60   30

Leeward - Norwegian Cruise Line
Bahamas/Mex (3/4)   Nor   Int   950   400

Legend of the Seas - Royal Caribbean Cruise Line
Alaska/Panama(7)   Nor   Int   2000   730

Leonid Sobinov - Baltic Line
Eur (14)   Rus/Ukr   Rus/Ukr   900   400

Lev Tolstoi - Black Sea Shipping (see Transocean Reederei)
Eur (various)   Ukr   Rus/Ukr   290   150

Lili Marleen - Deilmann Reederei
Carib (various)   Ger   Eur   50   30

Maasdam - Holland America Line
Alaska/Carib (7)   Dut   Fil/Ind   1600   590

Majesty of the Seas - Royal Caribbean Cruise Line
Carib (7)   Nor   Int   2700   800

Marco Polo - Orient Lines
Asia (various)   Eur   Fil   900   350

Maxim Gorki - Belata Shipping Company
Eur (various)   Rus/Ukr   Rus/Ukr   780   340

MegaStar Aries - Star Cruise
Southeast Asia (6)   Sca   Fil   70   35

MegaStar Taurus - Star Cruise
Southeast Asia (6)   Sca   Fil   70   35

Meridian - Celebrity Cruises
Bermuda/Carib (7-11) Gr   Int   130   580

Mermoz - Paquet French Cruises (Croisieres Paquet)
Carib/Eur (14)   Fr   Fr/Ind   660   320

Mikhail Sholokhov - Far Eastern Shipping Company
S.Pacific (various)   Rus/Ukr   E.Eur   400   170

Minerva - Swan Hellenic Cruises (see P & O)

Ship	Itinerary	Officers	Crew			
Minerva	Various	Gr	Gr	450		200

Monarch of the Seas - Royal Caribbean Cruise Line

	Carib (7)	Nor	Int	2700		820

Monterey - Starlauro Cruises

Eur (4-11) It Int 630 280

Nantucket Clipper - Clipper Cruise Line

US/Canada (7-14) Am Am 100 40

Neptune - Epirotiki Lines

Aegean (3/4) Gr Gr 200 100

Nieuw Amsterdam - Holland America Line

Alaska/Carib (7) Dut Fil/Ind 1300 540

Nippon Maru - Mitsui OSK Line

Asia (various) Jap Jap 600 160

Noordam - Holland America Line

Alaska/Carib (7) Dut Fil/Ind 1300 530

Nordic Empress - Royal Caribbean Cruise Line

Bahamas (3/4) Sca Int 2000 670

Norway - Norwegian Cruise Line

Bahamas/Carib (7) Nor Int 2300 880

Ocean Breeze - Dolphin Cruise Line

Bahamas (3/4) Int Int 940 380

Ocean Majesty - Majestic International Cruises

Med (7) Gr Gr 530 230

Oceanic Grace - Oceanic Cruise (Showa Line)

Asia (various) Jap Int 120 7 0

Odessa - Black Sea Shipping (see Transocean Reederei)

World (various) Rus/Ukr Rus/Ukr 570 250

Odysseus - Epirotiki Lines

Eur (3-7) Gr Gr 480 200

Olympic - Epirotiki Lines

Med (7) Gr Gr 620 230

Oriana - P & O Cruises

World (various) Bri Int 1900 760

Orpheus - Epirotiki Lines

Eur (14)	Gr	Gr	300	140

Pacific Princess - Princess Cruises

World (various)	Br	Int	700	350

Polaris - Special Expeditions

World (Exp)	Swe	Fil	80	40

Princesa Amorosa - Louis Cruise Lines

Med (3/4)	Gr	Int	300	130

Princesa Cypria - Louis Cruise Lines

Med (3/4)	Gr	Int	600	200

Princesa Marissa - Louis Cruise Lines

Med (3/4)	Gr	Int	700	230

Princesa Oceanica - Louis Cruise Lines

Med (3/4)	Gr	Int	500	220

Princesa Victoria - Louis Cruise Lines

Med (2/3)	Gr	Int	650	330

Queen Elizabeth 2 - Cunard Line

World (various)	Br	Br/Int	1800	1000

Queen Odyssey - Royal Cruise Line

World (various)	Nor	Eur	210	130

Radisson Diamond - Radisson Seven Seas Cruises

Carib/Med (4-7)	Fin/Am	Am/Int	350	190

Regal Empress - Regal Cruises

Bermuda/Carib (2-7)	Eur	Int	1160	350

Regal Princess - Princess Cruises

Alaska/Carib (7)	It	Int	1900	700

Renaissance I-VIII (8 sister ships) - Renaissance Cruises

Various (7)	It	Eur/Fil	100	70

Rhapsody - Starlauro Lines

Med (7-15)	It	Int	950	350

Romantica - Paradise Cruises

Med (3/4)	Gr	Int	720	190

Rotterdam - Holland America Line

Alaska/Carib (7+)	Dut	Fil/Ind	1200	600

Royal Majesty - Majesty Cruise Line
Bahmas/Bermuda (3-7) Gr   Int   1500   520

Royal Odyssey - Royal Cruise Line
Various   Gr   Gr   820   430

Royal Princess - Princess Cruises
Various   Bri   Int   1250   520

Royal Star - Star Line Cruises
Indian Oc (4-15)   Gr   Eur   250   120

Royal Viking Sun - Cunard Line
World (various)   Nor   Eur   800   460

Russ - Far Eastern Shipping Company
Baltic/Med (7-14)   Rus/Ukr   E.Eur   400   170

Ryndam - Holland America Line
Carib/Eur (7)   Dut   Fil/Ind   1600   590

St. Helena - Curnow Shipping
Wales-S.Afr (27)   Bri   Bri   120   40

Sagafjord - Cunard Line
World (various)   Nor   Eur   620   350

Sea Breeze I - Dolphin Cruise Line
Carib (7)   Gr   Int   1250   400

Sea Cloud - Sea Cloud Cruises (see Deilmann Reederei)
Carib/Eur (7)   Ger   Eur   60   60

Sea Goddess I - Cunard Line
Carib/Eur (7-11)   Nor   Sca   110   90

Sea Goddess II - Cunard Line
Eur/Orient (7-14)   Nor   Sca   110   90

Sea Princess - P & O Cruises
Eur (14)   Bri   Bri   740   380

Seabourn Pride - Seabourn Cruise Line
Various (7-14)   Nor   Eur   200   140

Seabourn Spirit - Seabourn Cruise Line
Eur/Orient (7-14)   Nor   Eur   200   140

Seaward - Norwegian Cruise Line
Bahamas (3/4)   Nor   Int   1700   630

Seawind Crown - Seawind Cruises

Carib (7)	Gr	Eur	700	300

Seawing - Airtours Cruises

Med (7/10)	Nor	Int	970	320

Sensation - Carnival Cruise Lines

Carib (7)	It	Int	2500	920

Shin Sakura Maru - Mitsui OSK Passenger Line

Asia (various)	Jap	Jap/Fil	550	200

Shota Rustaveli - Black Sea Shipping

Eur (various)	Rus/Ukr	Rus	600	350

Silver Cloud - Silversea Cruises (see V-Ships)

World (various)	It	Eur	330	200

Silver Wind - Silversea Cruises (see V-Ships)

World (various)	It	Eur	300	200

Sir Francis Drake - Tall Ship Adventures

UK/Carib/US (3-7)	Bri	Int	30	15

Sky Princess - Princess Cruises

Alaska/Carib (7)	Bri	Eur	1350	550

Song of America - Royal Caribbean Cruise Line

Bermuda/Carib (7)	Nor	Int	1550	530

Song of Flower - Radisson Seven Seas Cruises

Ind/Eur (7)	Nor	Eur/Fil	200	140

Song of Norway - Royal Caribbean Cruise Line

Carib/Eur (various)	Nor	Int	1130	420

Southern Cross - CTC Cruise Lines

Various	Ukr/Eur	Ukr/Eur	720	270

Sovereign of the Seas - Royal Caribbean Cruise Line

Carib (7)	Nor	Int	2500	800

Sovetskiy Soyuz - Murmansk Shipping

Polar (Exp)	Rus/Ukr	Eur/Ukr	100	130

Splendour of the Seas - Royal Caribbean Cruise Line

Carib/Eur (12)	Nor	Int	1800	700

Star Aquarius - Star Cruise

Southeast Asia (2/3)	Sca	Fil	1900	750

Star Clipper - Star Clippers Inc.
Carib (7-14)	Eur	Int	180	70

Star Flyer - Star Clippers Inc.
Carib/Eur (7)	Eur	Int	180	70

Star Odyssey - Fred Olsen Cruises
Alaska/USA (7)	Gr	Int	790	330

Star Pisces - Star Cruise
Southeast Asia (2/3)	Sca	Fil	1900	750

Star Princess - Princess Cruises
Alaska/Carib (7+)	It	Eur	1620	600

Star/Ship Atlantic - Premier Cruise Lines
Bahamas (3/4)	Gr	Int	1600	550

Star/Ship Oceanic - Premier Cruise Lines
Baahmas (3/4)	Gr	Int	1500	530

Statendam - Holland America Line
Carib/Eur (various)	Dut	Fil/Ind	1600	590

Stella Maris - Sun Line Cruises
Med (7)	Gr	Gr	180	110

Stella Oceanis - Sun Line Cruises
Med (3/4)	Gr	Gr	360	140

Stella Solaris - Sun Line Cruises
Various	Gr	Gr	700	330

Sun Princess - Princess Cruises
Alaska/Carib (7)	It	Int	1950	900

Sun Viking - Royal Caribbean Cruise Line
Alaska/Carib (10)	Nor	Int	800	340

SuperStar Gemini - Star Cruise
Southeast Asia (7)	Sca	Fil	800	330

Symphony - StarLauro Cruises
Eur (6-11)	It	Int	660	330

Taras Shevchenko - Black Sea Shipping
Eur (various)	Rus/Ukr	E.Eur	700	370

The Azur - Festival Cruises
Eur (various)	Gr	Int	750	320

Triton - Epirotiki Lines
Med (3-7)	Gr	Gr	890	260

Tropicale - Carnival Cruise Lines
Alaska/Carib (7)	It	Int	1400	550

Universe - World Explorer Cruises
Alaska (14)	Chi	Chi/Fil	830	200

Veendam - Holland America Line
Carib/Eur (7)	Dut	Fil/Ind	1250	580

Victoria - P & O Cruises
Carib/Eur (14)	Bri	Bri/Goan	710	380

Viking Serenade - Royal Caribbean Cruise Line
Mex (3/4)	Int	Int	1860	600

Vistafjord - Cunard Line
World (various)	Nor	Eur/Asian	730	380

Vistamar - Mar Line (c/o Viamare Travel)
Med/S.Am (4+)	Spa	Eur	340	100

Westerdam - Holland America Line
Carib (7)	Dut	Fil/Ind	1770	640

Wind Song - Windstar Cruises
Fr.Polynesia (7)	Bri	Ind/Fil	150	90

Wind Spirit - Windstar Cruises
Carib/Med (7)	Bri/Dut	Ind/Fil	150	90

Wind Star - Windstar Cruises
Carib/Eur (7)	Bri	Ind/Fil	160	90

Windward - Norwegian Cruise LIne
Alaska/Carib (7)	Nor	Int	1450	480

World Discoverer - Society Expeditions
World (Exp)	Eur	Eur/Fil	130	75

Yamal - Murmansk Shipping
Ant/polar (Exp)	Rus/Ukr	Eur/Ukr	100	130

Yorktown Clipper - Clipper Cruise Line
US/Carib (various)	Am	Am	140	40

Zenith - Celebrity Cruises
Carib (7)	Gr	Int	1790	630

LANDLUBBER'S GLOSSARY OF NAUTICAL TERMS

Abeam	At or from the side of the ship
Aboveboard	Areas of the ship above the waterline
Accommodation ladder	External folding ladder, used to climb aboard the ship from a pilot boat, etc.
Aft	Near, towards or in the rear section of the ship
Alleyway	Corridor or passageway
Aloft	Above the ship's superstructure, such as at or near the masthead
Alongside	When the ship is beside the pier (or another vessel)
(A)midships	In or towards the middle of the ship
At anchor	When the ship is anchored offshore (as opposed to docking alongside)
Anchor ball	Black ball that is hoisted on the bow, to signify that the ship is at anchor
Astern	Behind the ship, beyond the stern
Avast	Stop
Backwash	Disturbed water, caused by propeller action when ship is reversing
Ballast	Extra weight in the hold
Bar	Sandbar, often caused by shoreline currents
Batten down	To secure open hatches or equipment likely to fall, while the ship is under way
Beam	Width of the ship at its widest point
Bearing	Compass direction from the ship to another object or location
Belowboard	Areas of the ship below the waterline
Berth	Docking space for the ship; also a bed inside the ship
Bilge	Spaces at the very bottom of the ship's infrastructure
Binnacle	Ship's compass
Bow	Front or most forward part of the ship
Bowthruster	Device to propel ship away from the quayside
Bridge	Centre of command and navigation (always at the front of the ship)
Bulkhead	Inner partitioning wall
Bulwark	Ship's outer wall
(To) Bunker	To take on fuel
Bunkers	Fuel storage area

Capstan	Large spindle for attaching or winding in ropes (hawsers) and cables
Cast off	Release ropes prior to departure
Chart	Navigational map
Cleat	Wedge-shaped device for making fast ropes (hawsers) or cables
Coaming	Raised lip on doorsills and hatches to prevent water from entering
Colours	Ship's emblem or flag of nationality
(The) Chief	The Chief Engineer
Comment cards	Forms filled in by passengers, as a means of rating the cruise
Companionway	Interior stairway
Course	Ship's direction (in degrees)
Cross alley	Alley crossing another (often used for bringing on stores, etc.)
D.S.	Abbreviation for Diesel Ship
Davit	Device for raising or lowering storage crates or lifeboats
Deadlight	Ventilated porthole cover
Deck(head)	Floor
Debark	Abbreviation of disembark
(To) Disembark	To leave the ship/go ashore
Dock	The act of bringing the ship alongside the dock, i.e. quay, berth or pier
Draft	Distance from the ship's waterline to the bottom of its keel
Embark	To enter or come on board the ship
Even keel	The ship in a true vertical position as opposed to listing to the side
F & B	Abbreviation of Food & Beverage
Fantail	The rear overhang of the ship
Fathom	Distance of depth (1 fathom = 6 feet)
Fender	Anything that cushions (protects) the ship's hull against the dock or other craft
Flagstaff	Flagpole on the stern of the ship
Fly/Cruise	Package deal consisting of flights to and from the ship as well as the cruise itself (also known as Air/Sea)
Fo'c's'le	Abbreviation of forecastle (section under the bow)
Fore	The front (bow) of the ship
Forward	Towards the front (bow) of the ship
Free port	Port or place exempt from customs duty
Funnel	Ship's chimney

Galley	Ship's kitchen
Gangway	Construction, ladder or ramp giving access to and from the ship
G.R.T. (grt)	Gross Registered Tonnage* (see end of Glossary)
Hatch	Cover leading to a hold
Hawse pipe	Large pipe in the bow holding the anchor chain or hawser (not to be confused with a hose pipe)
Hawser	Huge rope used for securing or towing the ship
Helm	Ship's centre of steering
Hold	Interior storage area towards the bottom of the ship
House flag	Flag denoting the cruise line to which the ship belongs
Hull	Framework (shell) of the ship
I.B.	Abbreviation for Ice-breaker
I.M.O.	Abbreviation for International Maritime Organisation, governing body for safety and other standards at sea
Inboard	Towards the centre of the ship (inboard cabins therefore have no portholes)
Jacob's ladder	Rope ladder (often with wooden rungs)
Keel	Longitudinal extension of the ship's underside, important for balance
Knot	Unit of speed (1 nautical mile per hour)
Landlubber	Anyone who is unfamiliar with life on the ocean wave
League	Measure of distance (1 league = approximately 3.5 nautical miles)
Leeward	Side of the ship that is sheltered from the wind
Line	Any rope that is smaller than a hawser
(To) List	To lean to one side (of drunken sailors as well as ships)
Log (book)	Ship's record of navigation, etc.
M.S.	Abbreviation for Motor Ship
M.T.S.	Abbreviation for Motor Turbine Ship
M.V.	Abbreviation for Motor Vessel
Maiden voyage	Ship's first official cruise
Manifest	List of passengers, crew or cargo
(To) Muster	(To) Assemble passengers and/or crew
Muster Station	Emergency assembly point
Nautical mile	Approximately 1.15 of a statute mile (6,080ft/ 1,870m)
(The) Old Man	(The) Captain (but never call him that to his face)
Open Sitting	Access (for passengers) to dine at any unoccupied

	table at any time during the restaurant opening hours (as opposed to an assigned table and dining time)
Outboard	Towards, at or beyond the ship's sides (therefore, outboard cabins usually have portholes)
Pax	Abbreviation for passengers
Pig (Pig & Whistle)	Crew Bar
Pilot	Independent navigational advisor at times of entering/leaving port, etc.
(To) Pitch	To rise and fall (of ship, especially in rough seas)
Plimsoll line	One of several marks painted on the ship's hull above the waterline to prevent overloading
Port	Left side of the ship
Port charges	Passenger charges and taxes which must be paid to government authorities in ports; these are normally included in the price of the cruise
Porthole	Circular ship's window
P.O.S.H.	Acronym for 'Port Out, Starboard Home', i.e. the more expensive cabin allocation on the England-India route
Prow	Bow of the ship
Quarterdeck	Rear section of the upper deck
Quay	Dock, pier or berth
Rating	Non-officer position/rank
(The) Ratings	Overall grades determined by the scores given by passengers on their comment cards at the end of the cruise
Repositioning Cruise	Interim itinerary taking the ship from one season's route to another
Rudder	Fin-like steering device below the waterline
Running lights	Three lights (green on the starboard, red on the portside and white at the top of the mast) that must be lit if the ship is sailing at night
S.S.	Abbreviation for Steam Ship
S.T.R.	Abbreviation for Steamer
Screw	Ship's propellor
Scuppers	Deck drainage system
Shake-down Cruise	Ship's unofficial first cruise, to sort out problems (at least in theory) before the official Maiden Voyage
Shell door	Outer opening above water level, enabling access for stores, pilots, passenger gangways, etc.
Sitting	Allocated passenger dining time i.e. first (earlier) or second (later) sitting
(The) Skipper	(The) Captain

Sounding	Measurement of water depth
Stabilizer	Gyroscopic retractable fin on either side of the ship to minimise rolling motion
Stack	Ship's funnel or 'chimney'
(The) Staff	Staff Captain
(The) Staff Chief	Staff Chief Engineer
Starboard	Right side of the ship
Stern	Back (or aft) of the ship
Stow	To load with cargo or provisions
T.B.A.	Abbreviation for To Be Assigned (cabins, etc.)
T.S.	Abbreviation for Twin Screw
T.S.S.	Abbreviation for Turbine Steamship
Tender	Small boat (often lifeboat) used to transport people to and from shore when the ship is at anchor
Transfers	Transport between the ship and airports, hotels, etc.
U.S.P.H.	Abbreviation for United States Public Health (inspection)
Under way	When the ship is about to depart
Wake	Trail of disturbed water behind a moving ship
Watch	Period (usually of 4 hours) spent on duty, not just watching
(To) Weigh anchor	To raise the anchor
Wheelhouse	Centre of navigation (the Bridge)
Windward	Side of the ship towards the wind
Working alley	Main passage in the crew area
Yaw	Deviation from the ship's course, generally caused by rough seas.

*A passenger ship's tonnage is calculated not by its actual weight, but by the total of permanently enclosed spaces, excluding the bridge, radio room and other specified areas. 1 GRT = 100 cubic feet of enclosed space, and is the basis by which port and other dues are calculated.

FAMILY TREE OF JOBS

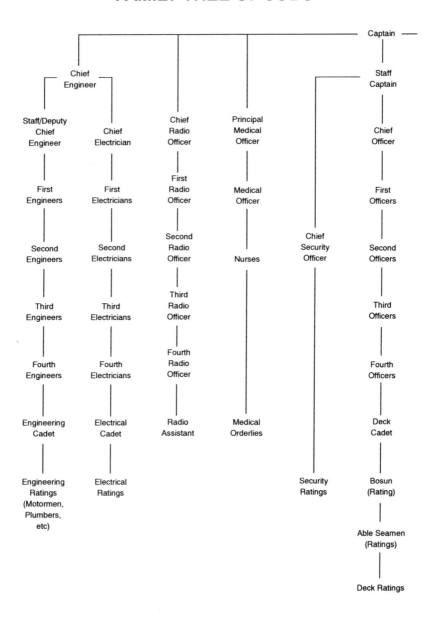

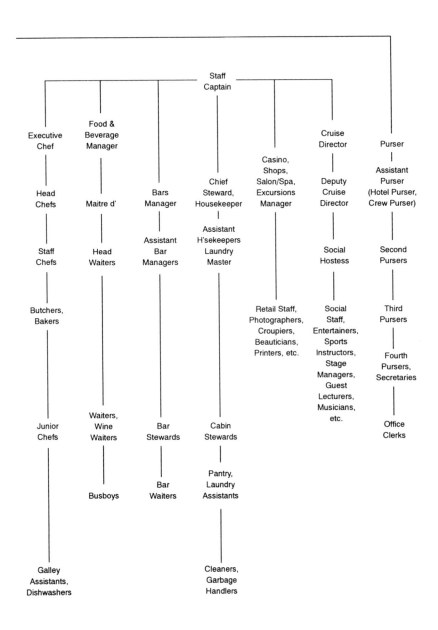

SAMPLE MENUS

LUNCHEON

APPETISERS

Devilled Eggs with Cornets of Ham

Gravlax
Salmon marinated in honey, dill and crushed pepper and served with a mustard-dill sauce

SOUPS

Cream of Spinach with Nutmeg

Beef Consommé with Tomato Bread Croutons

Chilled Strawberry and Vanilla Soup

EGG DISH

Mushroom Omelette with Watercress Garnish

ENTREES

Sautéed Fillet of Hake
with tomato concasse, served with saffron sauce

Breaded Pork Chops
Golden-fried, served with apple purée

Spaghetti al Pesto
with a pesto sauce of olive oil, pine nuts and basil, served with parmesan cheese

VEGETABLES

Carrots, Green Beans, Roast and Boiled Potatoes

CHEF'S HEALTHY OPTION

Beef Consommé

❖

Poached Fillet of Hake
served with steamed vegetables and boiled potatoes

❖

Fresh Fruit Salad

Luncheon cont'd

SANDWICH OF THE DAY

Tuna and Avocado Toasted Triple-decker
with mayonnaise, served with salad garnish and salsa

SALAD OF THE DAY

Chicken Caesar's
Freshly tossed Caesar's salad with strips of lean chicken, served with parmesan cheese

FROM THE GRILL

Grilled Ham and Cheese Toastie
served with french fries, coleslaw and green pickles

DESSERTS

Double Chocolate Cake
with chocolate sauce and vanilla ice cream

Blueberry Yoghurt Cream
with crushed blueberry sauce

Pecan Pie with Vanilla Ice Cream

ICE CREAMS

Vanilla, Chocolate, Neopolitan or Frozen Cherry Yoghurt

DESSERT SAUCES

Chocolate, Vanilla, Strawberry, Raspberry

ASSORTED FRESH FRUITS AND CHEESES

BEVERAGES

Full Roast or Decaffeinated Coffee,
Tea or Herbal Tea (Camomile, Mint, Rosehip)

DINNER

APPETISERS
Brazilian Hearts of Palm, served with Mustard Mayonnaise
Lobster and Crab Cocktail, served with Sauce Cardinal
Macedoine of Citrus Fruits in Grand Marnier

SOUPS
Cream of Cauliflower 'Dubarry'
Chicken Consommé with Vegetable Julienne

ENTREES
Sautéed (Boneless) Rainbow Trout 'Meuniere'

Prime Rib of Beef 'Bouquetiere'
served with horseradish sauce

Roast Turkey
served with chestnut dressing, giblet sauce and cranberries

Penne alla Puttanesca
*Pasta in a sauce of garlic, tomato, capers, olives, peppers and oregano,
served with parmesan cheese*

VEGETABLE ENTREES
Vegetable Quiche baked with Herbs and Gruyere Cheese

VEGETABLES
Carrots 'Vichy', Brussels Sprouts
Roast, Baked, Mashed and Parsley Potatoes

SALADS
Salad 'Aida'
Iceberg lettuce, artichoke, egg and peppers in a Dijonnaise dressing

Garden Salad
Lettuce, cucumber, tomato and carrot in a vinaigrette dressing

Dinner cont'd

CHEF'S SUGGESTION
Brazilian Hearts of Palm
Cream Soup 'Dubarry'
Roast Turkey
Apple and Raisin Pie

LEAN AND HEALTHY OPTION
Chicken Consommé
Penne alla Puttanesca
Sugar-Free White Chocolate Eclair

DESSERTS
Apple and Raisin Pie, served with Vanilla Ice Cream
Warm Ricotta Cheese Crepes, served with Raspberry Sauce
Creme Caramel garnished with Exotic Fruits
Selection of Ice Creams and Dessert Sauces

Tonight's Flambéed Speciality
Cherries Jubilee served with Vanilla Ice Cream and Cinammon

DIABETIC DESSERT
Sugar-Free White Chocolate Eclair

SELECTION OF CHEESES AND BISCUITS

SELECTION OF FRESH FRUITS

BEVERAGES
Full Roast or Decaffeinated Coffee,
Tea or Herbal Tea (Camomile, Mint, Rosehip)

AFTER DINNER MINTS

FURTHER READING

The following books will help you to become better acqainted with the world of cruising:

Berlitz Complete Guide to Cruising and Cruise Ships is an annually revised book aimed primarily at prospective passengers. But it also supplies a general insight into the world of cruising, together with comprehensive information on all the major lines and vessels. Published by Berlitz Publishing Company Ltd (Berlitz House, Peterly Road, Oxford OX4 2TX; and in US at 257 Park Avenue South, New York, NY 10010). The most recent edition retails at £13.95/$18.95 (US)/$23.95 (Canada).

Cruise Industry News Quarterly is an international magazine covering all areas of the cruise industry. Copies are available direct from their American office (441 Lexington Ave, Suite 1209A, New York, NY 10017). An annual subscription (including overseas postage) costs $40 ($26 in the US).

Cruise Travel is 'America's No. 1 Cruise Vacation Magazine,' a bimonthly publication containing articles and information about the cruising industry. Published in the USA by World Publishing Co, 990 Grove St, Evanston, IL 60201-4370 (tel: 708-491-6440). Annual subscriptions cost $18.00 in the US/$24 worldwide.

Cruises and Ports of Call is a book containing information on the major ships and lines and the most popular itineraries. Aimed at prospective passengers, it also provides interesting background reading for job hunters, especially for those seeking work in the shore excursion sector. Published by Fodor's Travel Publications (20 Vauxhall Bridge Road, London SW1V 2SA; also 201 East 50th St, New York, NY 10022, USA). The 1996 edition costs £14.99/$18.50 (US)/$25.50 (Canada).

Fielding's (Guide to) Worldwide Cruises is a yearly bumper paperback aimed at the potential passenger market, but including a lot of information about the ships, cruise lines and ports of call which may be relevant to potential employees. Published in the United States by Fielding Worldwide, Inc (308 South Catalina Avenue, Redondo Beach, CA 90277), it costs £11.95/$17.95 (US)/$23.95 (Canada).

Frommer's (Comprehensive Travel Guide) Cruises is also published with the passenger in mind. Again, this book gives useful information on cruise lines and itineraries that may also interest job seekers. Published in the United States by Macmillan Travel (15 Columbus Circle, New York, NY 10023), the 1996 edition retails in the UK for £12.99 and in the US and Canada for $19 and $23.50 respectively.

Jobs Afloat is published by a British employment agency and gives an update on current job availability on cruise ships and yachts. Contact Travelmate (52 York Place, Bournemouth BH7 6JN) for details.

Lloyds Register of Ships and *Lloyds Register of Shipowners* are both published annually by Lloyds Register of Shipping (71 Fenchurch St, London EC3M 4BS; tel: 0171-709 9166). Recent editions of this comprehensive global listing of ships and shipowners can be found in most good reference libraries.

The Motor Ship Directory contains names and addresses of shipowners, consultants, shipbuilders/repairers, engine builders, etc. Published annually by Reed Business Publishing Ltd (Quadrant House, The Quadrant, Sutton, Surrey SM2 5AS; tel 0181-652 8183); copies may be found in public libraries.

Overseas Jobs Express is a fortnightly newspaper, listing general work opportunities abroad, including those on ships. It is based at Premier House, Shoreham Airport, Sussex BN43 5FF, England (tel: 01273 440220). Subscriptions in the UK cost £19 for three months or £52 for 12 months.

Porthole is a bi-monthly cruise magazine, published by the author of the *Berlitz Complete Guide to Cruising & Cruise Ships*. For details, send a stamped addressed envelope to: Douglas Ward, *Porthole Magazine,* 10 Fairway Drive, Suite 200, Deerfield Beach, FL 33441-1854, USA (tel: 305-426-0046).

Sea Breezes is a long-established (since 1919) monthly magazine 'of Ships and the Sea', retailing at £1.95 and often containing features pertinent to the cruising industry. For subscription rates, contact *Sea Breezes Magazine,* Units 28-30, Spring Valley Industrial Estate, Braddan, Isle of Man IM2 2QS (tel: 01624 626018).

Shipping–Today & Yesterday is a monthly magazine, covering all areas of shipping including cruising, and retailing at £1.80 per copy. Subscription rates are available from the publishers: HPC Publishing, Drury Lane, St Leonard's-on-Sea, Sussex TN38 9BJ (tel: 01424 720477).

The Telegraph (not to be confused with the daily) is the newspaper of NUMAST mentioned above. It is not available through newsagents but is distributed to companies and colleges specialising in the maritime industry. Personal copies can be sent to your home address for an annual subscription of £9. Phone 0181-989-6677 for more details.

Travel Trade Gazette is a publication about the travel industry in general including cruising. It also publishes the annual *Travel Trade Gazette Directory* which includes addresses of cruise lines and operators and can be found in most public libraries in the UK. For more details, contact their Head Office at Riverbank House, Angel Lane, Tonbridge, Kent TN9 1SE (tel: 01732 362666).

There are also various 'How to Get Work at Sea'-type publications, available only by mail order, seen in the advertisement columns of newspapers. Some of these give some worthwhile information; many will be overpriced, and a few will be downright rip-offs. *Caveat emptor.*

Vacation Work also publish:

	Paperback	Hardback
The Directory of Summer Jobs Abroad	£7.99	£12.99
The Directory of Summer Jobs in Britain	£7.99	£12.99
The Teenager's Vacation Guide to Work, Study & Adventure	£6.95	£9.95
Work Your Way Around the World	£9.95	£15.95
Working in Tourism – The UK, Europe & Beyond	£9.99	£15.99
Working with the Environment	£9.99	£15.99
Teaching English Abroad	£9.95	£15.95
The Au Pair & Nanny's Guide to Working Abroad	£8.95	£14.95
Working in Ski Resorts — Europe & North America	£8.95	£14.95
Kibbutz Volunteer	£7.99	£12.99
The Directory of Jobs & Careers Abroad	£9.95	£15.95
The International Directory of Voluntary Work	£8.95	£14.95
The Directory of Work & Study in Developing Countries	£7.95	£10.95
Live & Work in France	£8.95	£14.95
Live & Work in the USA & Canada	£8.95	£14.95
Live & Work in Australia & New Zealand	£8.95	£14.95
Live & Work in Scandinavia	£8.95	£14.95
Live & Work in Germany	£8.95	£11.95
Live & Work in Belgium, The Netherlands & Luxembourg	£8.95	£11.95
Live & Work in Spain & Portugal	£8.95	£11.95
Live & Work in Italy	£7.95	£10.95
Travellers Survival Kit Lebanon	£9.99	–
Travellers Survival Kit: Russia & the Republics	£9.95	–
Travellers Survival Kit: Western Europe	£8.95	–
Travellers Survival Kit: Eastern Europe	£9.95	–
Travellers Survival Kit: South America	£12.95	–
Travellers Survival Kit: Central America	£8.95	–
Travellers Survival Kit: Cuba	£9.99	–
Travellers Survival Kit: USA & Canada	£9.95	–
Travellers Survival Kit to the East	£6.95	–
Travellers Survival Kit: Australia & New Zealand	£9.99	–
Hitch-hikers' Manual Britain	£3.95	–
Europe – Manual for Hitch-hikers	£4.95	–

Distributors of:

Summer Jobs USA	£9.99	–
Internships (On-the-Job Training Opportunities in the USA)	£15.99	–
Sports Scholarships in the USA	£12.99	–
The Directory of College Accommodations USA	£5.95	–
Emplois d'Ete en France	£7.99	–
Making It in Japan	£8.95	–

Vacation Work Publications, 9 Park End Street, Oxford OX1 1HJ
(Tel 01865-241978. Fax 01865-790885)